The Hard Road

A humble book of prose and bullshit.

By Sam Sanborn

<u>A foreword or 45</u>

you can tell yourself
    all kinds of things
        but the only true form
            of knowledge
                stems from indifference
    and diligence.

        the question "why?"
        keeps you impotent.

        the question "how?"
        keeps you stagnant.

so the only
    question
        that remains
            is

        "what comes next?"

        and the journey begins!

You see, the devil haunts a hungry man
If you don't want to join him, you got to beat him
I ain't sayin' I beat the devil, but I drank his beer for nothing
Then I stole his song.

And you still can hear me singin', to the people who don't
listen
To the things that I am sayin', prayin' someone's gonna hear
And I guess I'll die explainin' how, the things that they
complain about
Are things they could be changin', hopin' someone's gonna
care.

I was born a lonely singer, and I'm bound to die the same
But I've got to feed the hunger in my soul
And if I never have a nickle, I won't ever die ashamed
'Cause I don't believe that no one wants to know.

-Kris Kristofferson

eye of the storm

There's nothing left to do.
From the petulantly reckless intake
of booze, cigarettes, pills and
the mother Mary, cast like shadows
over the charred innards strewn
haphazardly over a rusting
merry-go-round, to the caustic
glances cast into flitting streams,
targeting the eddying pools ripe
with all manners of sustenance
and murk, this crumbling shanty
of folds has failed, in every tense
and pretense, to rectify any type
of error, any misplaced 1 or 0, or
make any head
way.

She. Isn't that how it always
begins? With that venomously sweet
connotation. With that dull ache that
bubbles and boils and burns and
boisterously blathers, blockading the
more tangible obstructions of thought
and manner. Isn't that the word that
rips you apart.
She did, and hardly knew it. It should
have been easier. The ship I have patched,
made sea-worthy and stocked with enough
provisions to make it
to that island, crest the peak
of that wave, etch lines in the forgiving
facade of permanence,
trembles in the neap tide, begging
me to say the words, pleading to take
another chance, to set out over the
waters in another attempt

to clear the water,
so to speak.

My friend, my comrade, my ally, this
barnacle encrusted shell of polished plexiglass
will never cease to amaze
the equally cracked and crusted dock workers
turned repairmen. This ship will sail till
the water succumbs. And we all know that
permanence has never bowed to the
feeble meanderings of man.
And we all know, by now, that a Captain goes down
with her.

With the ship, I mean.

She used to smile when I said that, one hand
at midnight on the wheel, the other stroking her
exposed thigh. She'd reach over and buckle me
anyway.

It's been a while. A long while. Over 100 poems
and catastrophic stories, over enough panties to
drown in, over 9000 maladaptive tendencies and
streams of consciousness.
For what, I cannot say. The trenchancies of love?
The idealistic wonderland that is so hard to kiss
goodbye? The damnation that has become ever more
appealing as it becomes ever more apparent?
Just another perfect storm? Another wave
to teach me some lesson that has gone unsung
for scarcely a second over millenia
by every cell in my being?

Is this just a wake up call? Or is it a pang
of something gruesomely real; the mistake
that spawned the regret that dawned the realization
of something infinitely and unbelievably

impermeable?

I'm going to hedge with the latter, whichever one
that is.
There's nothing left to do, anyway.
This ship, resurrected, still floats.
This captain, oxidizing fast, still stands.
And the clock remains shattered beneath
untold gallons.

And I'm starting to like it that way.

she's a smooth glass of water
a breeze that blows into the room
and lifts your eyebrows
as if they had been sagging, like grapes
from the vine. she
blows you a kiss and smiles
bubbling like champagne,
bursting like buds at dawn.
I grin a boy's grin,
suddenly confident and beaming,
rising without speaking
to take her hand and run
right out the front door.

My name is Sam.

When the crusty streets make you
want a drink
and you've tossed
enough towels and headphones to
make Christmas look simple
and where you've gone through
two dozen pasty, disgustingly
compassionate shrinks
trying to soften the blow, warm up
the enema tube and inject you with
sugar, spice and everything nice
when you've wanted to scream till
your throat ruptures
for a decade
you find it important to ram the key
into the self destruct
that big red button
right under your nose
and let it all just fucking rip
tear and tend it's way
out of a carapace as hollow as your
war chest

I know now that the walk away in the
morning is not out of fear of
commitment, it is out of a resistance
toward having something to lose
and those martyrdoms, heroic underpinnings
are lost in the chorus
of how much of an asshole you must
be yet you must be.

See the thing is that everything is not
going to be alright for everyone and to
think so ignores the billions of
people fighting for their lives

their minds
their daughters
their ill-conceived, pragmatic
nightmares
and their ex-wives
we have to coalesce our ideals with
shuttered, rosy shades in order to
fool ourselves into smiling
much more than we deserve.

And there is a little 13 year old girl
inside of all of us
that keeps wailing
"it's so hard"
and those transferred voices of all
of those people pretending to listen
saying get the hell off stage
and your own, tiny little voice
internally pressing the detonation
switch the aforementioned, the holy
fuck potatoes Mr. Magoo there's no
turning back now
you are fucked if you give in to the
fear of not saying anything at all
hell
you'll get fucked anyway
and it all comes together in one big
cacophony of booze and
microphone tyranny, just one more
dictator of time and sound,
an impermanent transference of every
tiny wave that crashed against my
shores breaking through the damn
and goddamnit
I have to say it all.

But still, roses smell really fucking
good in the sun and IPAs make it all

bearable and every once in a while
pale, freckled gingers with horse
faces and pointy ears get beautiful
women to smile
and sometimes even take them
home
and sometimes no one finds reason
to pick you apart for
no reason and sometimes it's
all genuinely good
under the hood.

But why is it that I can't go ten
minutes without stopping
somewhere for a drink and moving
moving
moving
on
towards something that I can't
define
and towards something I can't pay
for till an illusory paycheck
smattered in powder and
shame
slathered in irregular heartbeats
fluttering down between
lesbians hitting on you at the bar
guy bartenders with eye makeup
and $3 gyros from the girl that craves
15 inch dick.

I just can't define it.

I just can't get enough here
enough beer
shots
cigarettes
steps

grease
exclamation marks
scars
butterflies
maps
winks
fucking tinder accounts
or time to live
to pack into one
day.

It's amazing how alone you can be
elbow to elbow with all kinds
of beautiful people
just one
well put together poker face
over a body left to ruin
and we wonder why they never call
back
the guitar plays
the people talk
nothing changes
and you're still alone
the shot and beer and cigarette
the flippant butterflies
the only things keeping you any kind
of company
as if anyone needed it
as if we didn't get into this company
for exactly the same
as if these drinks weren't purely medicinal
and as if we weren't completely
addicted to everything we wished
we didn't attribute to instinctually
actually
distinctly
unintellectually
simply.

And all I want to do is vanish
poof
like the sand blown from the
fingertips of a gypsy palm reader
but you can't take the easy way out
because of this Christmas gift of life
hung up over the mantle and
positively dripping with soot and ash
so you flirt with pretty girls
and volunfuckingteer
and wait wait wait
I can't fucking wait
to quit this job
kick rocks
make trails
catch them on the flipside
see, you know you will never grow
moss
when you never know people for
longer than a few months
their loss
send my w-2s
on time
please.

see, this whole living and breathing
thing
is just a tragic comedy
full of dancing shoes
10 ways to smile
inspirational quotes from people
who ended up shooting themselves
and a hell of a lot of calls to your
brothers and mothers
excuse me, is this thing on?
because Burning in Water, Drowning
in Flame is not just the half cocked

derivation of a drunk miser left to his
own obsolete devices
rather it is a template for how to boil
in your own skin
laid down on papyrus with indigo dyes
it's a blueprint for disaster and a
harbinger of the greatest kind of
successful failure.

but goddamnit those roses smell
good in the heat
don't they?
and how can you not love the sound
of high heels on marble floors
and sometimes there are gems in the
rotten hay we reap
till death do we part
maybe there really is something in
store
so buckle your seat belt young man
you're gonna get what you deserve
and because the devil would never
let your death stand
you might as well drift the curves
drink the rain and splash in puddles
take off into an interchangeable
unknown, promise
a confession of doubts gone realities
and the city slicker
malaise
tossed over a shoulder
laden with manufactured
portable residency
fades
into words
as the big red button on the console
smack dab in the middle
of the bridge

presses itself
and the Captain slowly closes the hatch
of the last escape pod
and punches
out.

fernweh

it itches
somewhere between brow and balls
a slight quake that urges, pleads
begs the question
why
why do I have to move
can't just stay
hang around
get to know them
        or it
                or her.
Why do I self-destruct
at the teeniest notion of permanence?
It's almost as if
that
this pursuit of meaning
gleans nothing
if not actualized in the form
of pictures taken
and a map of these locations
pinned to the wall
of women laid
mountains conquered
highways skated

friends
made and left.
Why is that nothing
is more important?

The women I've fortunately
met have unanimously
claimed the same concept
of why
oh why
do you have to move
so fast?

I cannot answer, rather
I have to untangle their
legs, arms, tongues,
hand in my keys
and raise mine
to hail the first taxi
out of there
a dichotomy of bipolarity
the pulling of opposite
yet equal forces
those of loss and gain
missing and found
life through steps taken
over and over
to over
again.

It's almost as if/just as if
the mind is only truly cleared
in movement
exactly the reason I used to run
just one ragged breath after another
to escape the pervasive self-loathing
the permeable gray layers
turning on themselves

but temporarily vanquished
as wheels turning
and experiences gained
compiled as miles.

It's almost as if/just as if
a life
that vehemently requires
trying every single possibility
twice
necessitates scurrying through;
as if the individual
experiences that define us
need to be had
as full automatics
sometimes need to be fired:
all in a blazing glory of
life, trajectory, and death
birth, rebirth, transference
and finally,
an evolution
into
of an
idea that exists everywhere
and anywhere
all at once
just like a feeling
of closing this book
pocketing this pen
and strutting away from
this beach
to a future
uncertain only in possibility
yet certain in each step taken
away and wondering.

way to go

The only thing I'd ever fallen through
with was the word goodbye
clean and easy
mean and simple
just one foot in front of the other
headphones plugged in
and off, atlas on the front seat
coffee adamantly steaming
up through the piles of butts
and the two half full beer cans
sweating in the cold air
blasting through the speakers.

I'd always half-assedly
tried to follow
the path of those who demonstrated
how to have no plan, no walkway
no place to sleep
and a pair of balls big enough to have
such a universally despised personality
with the same vagabond mentality
of those with much more congenial
outlooks.

One bed. Smoking, please.

There is probably very little difference now,
aside from a hot losing streak
so commonplace in the mundanities of the
service industry that an entire generation
has found themselves thoroughly entrenched in,
as if we were the first middle class
raised for a life in the trenches of a mental battle
waged across the world wide web, Greyhound benches,
and those prevalent, fluorescent street signs
glistening in the rain.

The only thing I'd ever followed through with
was the obedience to that oh-so-pervasive voice
smoothly and efficiently goading me to
"run. Run. RUN!" away from those overbearing
maladaptive tendencies and the compulsory
attendance at those watering holes
marked in every corner with the acrid scent
of failure
of grim determination
and of those staunch defenders of the right to breathe
through and out of all those things
our mothers didn't mention
would happen during our days.

It's a good thing this country is an oblong sphere,
just a series of deep cuts across a ragged landscape
those tributaries in which inevitably
sluice you straight back home
with the subtle tickle of a high tide
nipping at your heels and poop deck
swabbed by the walking eulogies
oft maligned and never internally understood
might as well have DOA on each toe
tattooed with matching phrases
"I'm Sorry"
on foreheads hiding behind
weeds and cast off bicycle parts
just drifting through crowds of woebegones
accepting bills that cannot be paid
and ultimately jet-setting to a restless
finality ever present in falling through
life one bus, car, pair of boots
at a time.

Sunshine

Early in the day she says that I look like a girl; that
I don't look cool without my sunglasses.
She hands me a gummy, telling me that while she is
almost out of them, someday her Mommy will go to the bank
pull money out of the shiny machine
and then she'll have more to share.

Her favorite color is pink and purple.

She is kicking me and hitting me
exacerbating all of the things she doesn't understand
yet that she feels through the innate energies
of the world constantly making her older,
stringier, gaunter. Someday the world will
keep her that skinny.

We're standing in a run-down coffin of a trailer.
I'm pulling pork,
tearing apart butts with my bare hands
a side job I picked up off the internet,
somehow both just for the weekend and for life,
while she dangles her legs off of a case of bottled water
toes reaching into midair, toying with the swirling
heat and smoke that barges into the opened doors
with every stray bit of breeze.

And here I am, playing babysitter to this impossibly sweet
Sunshine, that's what I call her, if only because she
lights up my face. She reminds me of what I strive to
be, of what I strive to attain in this chaotic wasteland
of greed and stress-induced familihood.

It's her Mother's 40th birthday and she's
choking in dust at a run-down fair, hustling ribs
and 9 dollar buckets of fries smothered in nacho cheese.

Living the Dream.

She has five daughters that she'll admit to
and obviously has no job.
Where the father is, well, that's another question
entirely, yet she smiles and carries on
hollering back orders as if she was born
for this.
She doesn't complain, even in the midst of an
obvious crisis, an obvious obliteration
of everything she'd hoped and dreamed for
simply to care for the slue of progeny
that she has to find a means of conveyance for,
a conveyor belt off of the track that she
found herself unwittingly on, as if she is
ridding the baggage carry at the airport,
hoping to get picked up by mistake.

During the tumult of turmoil that we call
the Dinner Rush it all falls apart.
The woman is homeless.
The family is looking at one another, wondering
when the hell they can get out of there.
I know I will never see either the woman,
her parents or Sunshine ever again.

I hope, for their sakes, that this is true.

Then the yelling starts and suddenly
the front trailer is all mine, the machinations
of a grease soaked wonderland,
the Big Time. I run the show until I can't take
it anymore, till the girl is crying and I am
near the frying point.
When another moon-faced teenager asks for
an extra large cheese fry I snap, whisk the
fructose corn syrup and saturated fat
grenade into a semi-palatable array and

walk the fuck out.

I hand a beer to her mother and pick up the girl.

And she's flying.
She's superwoman.
And all the cares, all the lacks,
everything is dissolved in the sea of people
flowing between the neon lights like water
through the dam.
She's giggling, reminding me how to laugh
a six year old's laugh
behind us are the broken adults
carelessly throwing away the tenets of civilization
of a fleeting happiness in a fleeting flicker of life
the kind that she is, by the grace of youth,
oblivious to.

She's flying, i'm holding her carefully by the ankles
too skinny, too frail, too narrow to support the weight
of what she'll inevitably fall back to
when I let her go
but for now she is free and giggling
and that's all I can do.

That's all this world is paying me
everything for.

Sunshine laughs, I laugh, the neon lights sparkle
and the fledgling night waits a minute
for the two sun-faced kids to
play superhero
amidst the mugging heat, flashing bulbs of summer
and those overbearing and incessantly falling
dust clouds.

those of us

can't remember the last
time I slept
my pen seems
to have a much better
understanding
of the when's, how's
why's
while I can only hold
why the fuck not
in any kind of snarled
8 pound test line
this is not a rampart
this is Balsa wood
just papermache
walls
keeping us from rupturing
more cranial wires
wrists and knees
and the occasional
jam band
thrown by gorillas
without the fucking glue
but the rock
growing bigger as I
lose recall
pushes us against
and they toss us aside
in cold, damp rooms
full of the disreputable
an inconceivable stank
and ultimately really fun
chaff of society
and we still exist
those of us
who hate models and
schools for ants

coinciding to a long
burned manifesto
452 degrees of charred opinions
those who couldn't even
flap their arms twice
to make pretend
at giving
flying fucks
about flimsy fences
and porcelain personalities
these are those
who can't sleep
listening instead
to the urgent murmurs
of pens
the disdaining glances
of a plastic rocket launcher
society
and their own inherent vices
until
they
or their pens
can figure out exactly
whether these walls
were erected to be broken
or whether
or not
they existed in the first place.

4 on Division

I gave up on the words early,
rationalizing a generalized laziness
and spewing forth those humdrum
pity-party excuses
that got me everywhere to nowhere
I wanted to be.
See, I was born with a caustic,
flame-laden tongue and burning eyes,
that vindictiveness that consumes
and the appearance of something
wholly unseen in congenial circles
of friends and families
gone wolfpacks.
I've come back time and time again,
to the words that make me whole,
that take away those nuances of character flaws
that shatter a pockmarked personality
already lit afire at birth.
Run on sentences decorate this expanse
of white
like budding grass on a shit smeared prairie,
if only because it's easier to shotgun words
than it is to prune freshly opened roses.
And while I may die in these fields
the fire that consumes them will breathe
me back into the lungs of the abyss
and I will be everything, everyone, everywhere.

Yes, I am back.

I feel the adrenaline rush behind every vowel.
My veins run heavy, as if they were made
of pliable steel.
My eyes dry and burn,
those well-worn rivulets run arid
as if droughting or doubting

the very appearance of the sun
shed down in pulsing waves over the slick,
freshly jackhammered pavement below.
The sun that I get up in the morning for.

See, I didn't think I'd make it another poem
gone rant gone treatise gone opus gone words
simply seeded into laconic faces. I thought
I would melt down those steel cords
keeping the shoulders and fingers from cannibalizing
one particularly pointy piece
chalked with gunpowder. I thought it would be the straw.

But there's one thing about being made of steel
no matter what they say or do,
no matter how much rain falls
and how much oxidation peels and uglifies my skin,
no matter your pathetic words and opinions,
no matter whether California stays attached to the mainland,
steel cannot be melted by overtime, booze, or opinion.

See, I gave up on the words
but they never for one second gave up on me.
So here I am, ready and willing,
to not just write them but rather, forge them.
Be them.
Try and break that.

I'll write your epitaph.

Bozeman

Again with the hurry up
gitty up
again with the cops
making demands
handing me tickets
taking my life for a ride
just GTA without gloves
friends lost, friends regained
struggle away like caterpillars
lost on a branch
that should have held olives
but rather just dropped
those little spinny things
as if shooting off
escape pods.

See there's one thing I know
aside from the tantalizing truth
inherent in every second in love
is that empires falter and fade
these days pass by
suddenly i'm old
and the transient properties
once potential
now kinetic
explode onto your eyes
your face
and your reality
as if melting icebergs
we thought were long past the realm of ever
crushing a valley or two.

Where we go
once the lights have dimmed
and the bars been overturned
is up to one's vindication

or is that one's mother's opinion?
No
more like appetite and vindication
and the cheap whiskey that
keeps you from your dreams
of cheaper bars
with cheaper currencies
and trains across
an expanse we can only drunkenly
dream of
as if pining for the end.

See we are just the nomadic antipathies
transferred into living, breathing
misanthropes for the cause
villains with hearts of gold
those fallen
through cracks established
in the 50's and hammered into the fibers
of a crumbling cement capitalistic fantasy
complete with white wicker fences
and the illusory dream
of doing what you love and still
having more money than everyone else.

See, we chose to breath.
We chose to give it all away
for that one moment atop the mountain
in our backyard
that one inch of powdery snow
who needs cocaine
those relentlessly pounding waves
on the beach
next to the hotels
we can't afford
but don't give two shits
to stay in anyway.

See, we gave away those force fed dreams
a pledge of allegiance to everything
they told us not to do,
not to say,
not to be.
There's only one finger
we'll ever need
and one more paycheck
till we can move again,
this Friday
we'll all eat so
fucking
well.

See, there's a religion non-crafted
in the fires of something they
want you to believe
and a fire in a belly
that breaks windows
when it is right and proper and
just crazy enough
to make this entertaining,
so here's a gitty up
again with the bags and tickets and tape
and goodbyes casually crossed across
tables of eggs and empty shot glasses
tilted rakishly
to an uncertain midday bus ride

So here's that escape pod,
littered with V8, apologies, branches
and of course
the bumper stickers of everywhere
you've been fired from
good luck in your office,
i've got some more
everything
to breath and drink and die off

and definitely,
without
one
shred
of doubt,
some more trouble to find.

broken hands

i've got two broken hands
and a beer battered soul
so these words continue to
appear as the the keys click
in that familiar tone and the
world just waits a minute
for me to get this down.

there's nothing i can tell you
that you can't figure for
yourself
but i can illuminate past
transgressions in the hopes that
you might not have to go
through all that
and by the by
have to tell me
all about it.

let's spare the swollen structures
the frayed sinews, the black cloud
coursing its way through bone fragments

all the way to the tender, unbroken,
part of my palm.
let's just
give it a rest.

this is nothing
but an exercise
in futility, two hands
slitting through the air
towards harder molecular structures
hopeful like David, caustic like acid
a heavenly bile spewing
its way from every disillusioned pore, just the
stream against the rocks;
eventually it will all
wash, wash, wash
away.

somehow the hands that feed me,
that jettison syllables into a
solipsistic stratosphere smattered
with the sinister sneers of
brilliant white paper
like mortars onto starry soldiers
they ache and whine, old men
trapped between the confines of tautly drawn
flesh, still
just pining for dirt.

too bad, my friends.
you're going to
have to heal
yet again, this is just the
second round and this
son of a bitch
ain't so tough and
there are minds on things
these fingers can't touch

and i'm lost in the collective
nightmare of trying to
figure out
just how asleep
and just how broken
i really am.

<u>let's play a game</u>

She walked away to the sound of her ballet shoes softly
alighting on the puddles, sloshed through a brain-y gray pulp,
pulling apart the folded pages as if peeling petrified onions.
For some reason it was the shoes that captivated me, two
fluttering birds attached to pale flowers, flitting back and
forth in some sort of cabalistic dance. The streets were
narrow and the night was cold. It seems pointless to say that it
was raining; it's always raining here. It's almost as persistent
as the women you can find at every pseudo-upscale bar in
town, cobra-eyed jackals fiending for a ring, an SUV and three
little reasons to hate you for. Only difference is: one you
ignore, the other ignores you.

A sign across the street read "PBR - $1".

I stood there watching those shoes rise and fall. Rise and fall.
Rise and fall. Soon the sound of sloshing and the quick,
smacking claps of her heels faded into the dull pattering of
water onto cement, aluminum and the dissolving leaves. For a
minute I battled the notion of smoking a cigarette. I'd been
trying to quit, a notion as absurd as the Earth being flat or
Disney pumping out talented artists. You could say that I had
an affinity toward weighing the costs and benefits of each

delicious infusion of cancer into my bloodstream. This particular debate lasted roughly 3.44489 seconds.

A sign across the street read "I miss my lung, Jack."

"Shit," someone mumbled "you got an extra one of those?"

I handed one over in the direction of the voice. I was still staring down the street where she had walked off without pausing, without throwing up even the laziest middle finger to call my own. Just plain inconsiderate. The voice sounded rough. Crusty, stretched to breaking, callous, an uncleaned pipe that's seen too many seasons of mold drenched air and soggy aftershocks. I know what's inside that voice. There was no reason to look, so I continued to stare down the street. The rain came down.

A taxi drove by, its window rolling down as it slowed to a crawl. Like a scene out of a movie the downpour picked up, sending little rivulets of grime down the back of my neck. Gaia's sweat, for less. Everything must go. I saw my breath charge out into the fray as gray fractals blossoming over the cement façade of city, only to learn a different point of view from the passing drops. If you can't beat 'em, evaporate. That's the American way. My cigarette's posture got worse by the second, drooping down toward the puddles of oil and vinegar accumulating under my shoes.

"You're PA-the-TIC!!!!" She screamed out the window, her face no doubt contorted with reckless piety and the scorn of a trillion women scampering away from history. "Get OVER yourself!!"

I wish there was a word for the sound of the tires as they kicked into action. It was like hearing paint scrubbed off the wall with a diamond ring, the chips of enamel reluctantly tumbling to the dusty floor. Then she was gone. I knew she was gone because I felt the hairs on the back of my neck return to my skin. I was still staring down that same patch of concrete, unable to comprehend the churlish beauty that had unfolded in front of my eyes. My hands ached for a pen and my mind ached for the strongest liquor I could get my hands on. My balls didn't want anything to do with either of them.

A sign on the corner read "Exotic Dancers! Free Well Drinks! Two-for-One Penicillin!"

"Dumb broads." Said the man, shuffling his feet audibly as he searched for his place amongst the water pillars. I still wasn't looking but I knew he was smiling. I suddenly realized that the man had been standing there for a considerable amount of time now, a fact that didn't disturb me in the least. The more down and out a man is the more empathy he can muster. You have to get your hands dirty to clean them. I realized he might have some wisdom, some kind words or an old adage he might be willing to share. Or a knife.

"Livin' on the Edge!" blasted like a snotrocket from the cracked window of a passing semi.
I turned to face the man and realized that I had been right. This guy hadn't just been beaten by the ugly stick; he had been beaten by the ugly stick's illegitimate child with that whore of a broom. He looked as if he'd been born in the water he was supposed to drown in and then flushed down the toilet in disgrace, only to pop up in the sink of the woman who decided to mother this unfortunate man. He was downtrodden, to say the least, his back folded by too many years of crack, heavy backpacks, and sleeping on his side under a bench. He smelled like the dumpster in back of the seafood buffet. Full. In the middle of a heat wave. I didn't hesitate.

"Do you like whiskey and tits?" I asked, finally tearing myself away from the captivating tunnel of the street. The man nodded. The mop of hair hanging over his brow jiggled, releasing a cascade of rain drops across the streaking oil.

Your battleship is sinking, Captain.
Cry me a submarine.

A sign across the street read "The best way to please the Lord is on your knees."

There was no way in Hell I was wasting any more time. Inside I went, the mangy shreds of filth shuffling along two paces behind me. The bouncer took one look at the attempted smile on my face and let us in. The eyes of every scantily clad woman with loose morals in the club immediately ratcheted to my wallet. Fresh meat. Pay day. I was just freckled gold; pink platinum. I walked around the back of the bar, snatched a bottle of Maker's and headed toward the stage. As I sat down I told myself that if I ever left that dank, molding strip club I would write the story. Tell the tale. Spin the web.

When I do, I'll make sure to send it to you.

definition of terms

Intermittent rain coats
bleary eyes
as the horn of the train
echoes through the Sacred
Valley, shaking our coffee
in time
to the rhythm of the
passing train tracks.

These people all have lives

nice boots
still working cell phones
and an understanding
that a real life
picture would look great
in the office.

They have a different
kind of motivation.

Paralyzed into movement
by the constant, incessant
wonder of "what if?"
the rest of us glaze the cake
slipping off ice imaginary
or real
caught in the net
with the rest of the catch
yet slippery enough to escape
and ride the train through
Holy pilgrimages
whenever the fuck we want.

Holiday Inn

so there's one thing more
just one
I swear
hello page
it's been a
bit
and there's this girl

yeah another poem
about the eternal struggle
to coexist with the need
the ephemeral pro image of
copacetic love
and the fucking booze
that keeps these tired arms floating
like fucking champions.
so
so
so
there's these new words
this brand spanking new
yet absolutely
fucking ancient concept
of finding that gem in the sand
and she's 20
fuck
I'm 26 going on 50
and I see the paths divergent
till they crack and bend like
boughs worth sleighing
hands worth laying
genres worth transgressing
this life seems to be just another
blatantly lucid chess game dream
and she seems to be the queen
worth knocking down
I can feel the walls slipping
as if Gandalf is walking the ramparts
and I still get up at 4
never sleeping
the paycheck may never come
yet there she is grabbing my hand
and I am pretending
please dont see me pretending
good god
just let me get out of here without

the scars
without the ancient battle wounds
that we all have across
hearts
hesitating to beat quite as
reluctantly
'cause I am here
I rule every second as a tyrant
of fun that no one saw
coming till she did
and I know I have to let her go
into the aether
but how can I forget the tangible and
corporeal love that only a man long
down the journey of petulance
could possibly understand
as if I could possibly grasp or
comprehend all of the goddamned
roads I've walked down without
looking back
thumb out
and everything I own
on my back
everything I regret coating my shoulders
and hips
just a new place
with a new feel
that seems to be love for the moment
and hey
I think I might be able to get one
second of a breather
I might just be able
to hide here for a minute
and good god I'm in
fucking love again
just another dumbshit human
lost along the road of pissing
shitting and drinking

as if I was any different
and that
this girl
wasn't the reason
I got up
yesterday
.

Phew.

print

back against a tree
sliding down some kind of erosion
into the reservoir beneath
in the fading light of a dwindling summer
the wind picks up the pages
and turns them for me
whether
I want them to or not.

hear,
I listened too intently
to the ideas and thoughts
of dead poets, warm fridges and boxcars
all just screeching and howling
that you better be good enough
to have something to say.

the reality is that these trails and dying trees
needed no introducing as seedlings
hardly even tossing their limbs now

to the frail bones and pale skin
of those who pay no mind to wood-faced
statues
we are all just clawing away through soil
anyway
might as well grab a pen
desecrate some off-maligned relative
and scratch, scratch, claw
my way back into the lower echelons
of pages gone roots
and words gone starting guns.

chiseling

all this time i hid
in my room, wasting my time and breath
scared of the inevitable
and foregone conclusion
of you falling in love with a man
i had yet to meet.

i see now
i see
just how true the long spoken words
dancing in front of red eyes
really are
if you love something, let it go
let her go
let her hop in that car and take off
smiling
as you hold back the tears by clenching
razor blades in your stomach

by flexing a stomach left turning
turning
turning into stone.

you can let your heart callous,
you can let off ballast
from a submarine pushing the waters
of a mid ocean fallacy,
it won't make her stay any longer
than she finds you fascinating as
watching a man spontaneously
crumble into sawdust.

all this time i tried to shape you
like play-doh into my own version
of you; into my own version of
a wife i didn't want.

as the door slammed in my face,
four times,
i crawled into the cavernous hole
spreading through my carapace like
an avalanche tumbling through the
maw of a volcano left
unstirred
and i burned as if caught in hellish fire
in the center of a two week
bolt of lightning.

she'll never be back,
and I sure as hell will
never carve a trail to Scranton
or Bellingham, Portland, LA, Bozeman
Creede, Bend, Londonderry, Tampa
Detroit, Austin, New Orleans, or Yosemite.
I will never find the time to go back to
Bogota
or ever come find you, straight backed and

sought after
in Taipei.
I will never come to your bar in Eugene.
I will never call you again
in Brooklyn
from Cannon Beach.

all this time I had such a
good idea
of what I wanted, and
needed needed needed
but the sharply cut chin
of the matter
is that these things that we
need need need
are just that and really
the only justifiable thing is
to listen to the words of the sages
and just
let her go
stand there, hands in pockets
as the car pulls out
go home and vacuum all of the hairs
off the pillow case
wash the back packs
throw everything in
sell what you can
you know what
with the rest
and get to steppin'
make those tracks
blaze a damn trail to nowhere
and put the stabbing, searing
memories of a wrenchingly recent past
in the churning dust
of the side of the road
in a state
you'd never admit to your mother

one thumb out
two tears dry on your sleeve
no longer hiding
nor idle
the moss no longer growing
on the face and reddening shoulders
of a man somehow turned
rolling a way
away
to another set of ears to push
the hair back into
all the while
counting minutes
till you have to repeat
the whole adventure over again
till you have to
wait wait wait
needing it all to go faster
as you slowly
gaining momentum now
look at how
GODDAMN FAST WE'RE GOING!!!
turn
spinning and solidifying
and there she goes
there
she
goes
into stone.

flat out, flat footed

This is seething,
the pound of awkward footsteps
hammered between the judgment
of eyes cast downward.
These poems do nothing
but fuel a cold, feckless fire,
as an auburn mop fumes and steams
at the back of a bus
rocking back and forth
to the rhythm of sinister heartbeats.

And I hate this mop, this man, this me,
as if that's any surprise
more than the situation
I put myself in.

Suddenly the world is red,
once a lush kingdom of green,
orange light cast from dopey street lights
avoiding my gaze
as if they are disappointed
for me.

This can't be the life I live.
I was supposed to be better.
Stronger.
Smarter.
Better.
I was supposed to be somebody.

Right?

big hammer, big words

what a fool
crouched, spine hanging
off the rotting porch
crumbling as he reads
Hemingway
and smoking, fuming, spewing,
rolls of cancer,
delirious in an attempt to
leave the house.

who wouldn't
chuckle and chortle
at the irony,
chasing such massive quantities
of anti-anxiety pills
with shaking hands
self loathing
and day old beer.

it's like watching through a
rust coated lens, sepia toned
and kaleidoscopic,
yet far too clear
for comfort.

this is like actually
being there.
who wouldn't smile
who wouldn't fucking BEAM
at such tireless efforts
to conform
just enough
to walk, walk, walk
through a glistening boulevard
of beautiful masks

hiding horrific obscenities,
at such a misappropriated
set of skills,
at pissing away another meaningless youth
and pushing the limits
of just how far
something can implode.

what a fool.

cheap flight cowboy

one more time
battle scarred, broke
ragged
this time internally limping
along to the new trap
shared room and bar
the only shining beacon
gesturing across the gaping
divide of the Atlantic
and exhausted
thoroughly
I stumble along
the East Coast
comfortably wired
on DD coffee
memories of curves
of sun, arms and winding
roads gone dreams
no longer deferred
and the understanding

that these skirts
and this world
haven't found a viable way
to kill me yet
so one more time
I resolutely fly
striving
just to show up
work back into health
and ultimately
make it all
happen again
as if this truly were
my first rodeo.

resolve

Caught up in it again
it caught me by the bones and shook
hard enough to rattle
a snake in a cold rage gobbling
a feral dog shaking the life
out of your orange tabby.

The rain mocked me
and I let it win.

I have a new race now,
but I remember the code
laced in irregular spirals
through every oasis of being
clinging to the vacuum

we call sentience.
I remember the streets that grip
running in ecclesiastic circles
I had thought they were holding
me back
when they were simply
holding
on
and I have not forgotten the glory
of the hills grounded
astride an electric fog
and the tense, urgent love of the pines
still burdened by the incipient drops
nor have I forgotten any of the faces
those that held the rope
either slipping or in iron talons
as I climbed those slashing mountains
and fell impossibly deep into the puddles
cast brilliantly on every stage.

How could one even begin to forget
the scars and laugh lines
when he is reminded with every breath
and word left unuttered
just exactly how far he has come and gone
to be somewhat here, to be
another galaxy of oases
caught adrift by the islands?

How could one delete the favorite moments
despite how brief they may seem
how much grief they may bring
or the effervescent tenaciousness
inherent in memories cast across
such a passably present state of mind.

I refuse to hold the grudges necessary
to maintain any sort of conscious

synaptical editing.
And I refuse to put any of the fingers
down for all the women I have had the fortune
of falling for nose first into such lusciously
smooth pavement.

A man can only be so lucky
so many times.

Still.

You can only count the passing train cars,
tightrope the overflowing gutters,
play so many games of scrabble
over coffee gone crack cocaine
run the same bars out of stock
and hide the overbearing flaws of character
that define you
so many times.

I could say that I was satisfied
but what's the use in lying to the page
as if it was
even listening
in the first place
I could also say that the mold and cardboard friends
hadn't found inroads through my nervous system
diluting the signals with false alarms
and leaving the entire system
a malfunctioning mess of myopsism.
What I couldn't say was that I could check
a certain love
and a ravenous hunger for something
to plug the rupturing core
sinking indiscriminately through
a very specific chest cavity.

I couldn't say that I'd succeeded.

90% of doctors agreed on the remedy,
The itchy feet given hiking boots.
One cried, three died and one simply stared
as I walked out of any semblance of love
that I may have ever been dreamed about
every night since.
With a mental machete I cut through this
manifest destination; this thickly wound
concrete jungle.
I may have lost my armor to the brambles
but I plunged the blade into the heart of the beast
and drank the blood till my eyes soaked
in the plasma of all that I am bound to be.
All that I will conquer.
For I am not fighting for my home anymore.
I am fighting for the space
to build a new one.

I'll just have to see you all
next time
                              I pass through.

                              here we go
another flight
another East Coast
transplant, blonde and skinny
an airport bar
buying the first round
as if chumming
kissing your cheek
here we go

wheels up, feet down
headphones and coffee
the portal
to another plane
of jettisoned existence
moving toward
another near miss
followed, always
by the bullseyes
that catapult you
we are nothing
inside the split second
between light and darkness
a towering human
pyramid of experience
hand held, crossed
cupped around plastic
we are the eternal
struggle
and we are moving
swirling backasswards
out of the bottle
to the book
everyone with any senses
left
can read, devour
castrate the fear of
and fertilize
as ideas drawn to
that flickering flame
it takes one foul burrito
and one air bubble
astride the plastic tube
to end
to rush with white
so take off
six trillion miles an hour
let us commercialize

our own rationalized
Fast Food Consciousness
till we finally sleep
again
only to wake
so grateful
for all of the airport
love on credit
new places
and stories worth
telling
here
we
go.

<u>stop quiz</u>

how do I get to these places
suddenly i'm stuck between
today and tomorrow and I can't
find a way to click my heels
to go home
but even then there's no place so
lonely as home
so yellow and blue as home
so vacant and unattended
so vividly barren and icy as home
I didn't couldn't shouldn't
have imagined that there was this
much distilled barley and grapes
and I'm back to feeling the slack on
my back where I want a belay cable

or a shotgun
I'm back to wanting
anything to take aside from this mildew
climbing its way past my hands and through
the blood to my brain
rendering it an abandoned stump in furies
abound like wildfires
till the vessels in my eyes burst
splattering my precocious hands
hanging as if handcuffed
in servitude.

I want to break the world surrounding me
ignoring the well-known fact that this
will bring a far more open place
than the first
deliriously trivial and retarding
one would think every environment
would taped off and flagged
but oh,
that would be much easier
than this rhetoric and
questions left open-ended.

big rock candy monster

as I sit
tacit as ever
a song comes on that I
don't hear often
anymore.

the jaunty guitar
teases my ears
for a moment
and
as the bearded tramp
whistles wistfully
for a mountain made
of candy and booze
the bittersweet
stench of nostalgia
rises up through
my blanching throat.

if only I could suffocate on
such a sweet
transgression.

I remember when
we used to stand
up against one
and all
screaming at the
top of our lungs and
challenging the
hordes of herds
to prove us wrong.
yes,
we said,
somewhere there is
a jail made of tin
and you can
walk right out
again
as soon as you are in.

we believed in
that.

in retrospect, it
wasn't such a
horrible idea.
but with
such 20/20 vision
comes a wretched transference
of occurrence.

how could I have known
what a
jail really was.
how could I have
possibly guessed
that everyone dies
and
somehow all
things
find their way
back
into the dirt.

I remember how
we used to
be fair and bright
like those goddamn
         lemonade springs,
sleeping beneath
empty box cars
never changing our socks
and laughing
the cold away.

now I sit
beneath a cigarette tree
with the breeze
carefully avoiding
my gaze,
remembering

all kinds of
tremulous trials
and
one particularly
telling
example.

as I drift,
wistfully strumming a
crumbling guitar, it
becomes ever more clear
that after the fruit
is squeezed and pulped and
all that
is left
amongst the wreckage of
vitality
are
the wretched pangs of
regret
and
candy coated memories.

ahoy

a bird shit on my
head today, in the park
I was
poised on the rusting frame
of
a derelict from the thirties
and

I was riding shotgun
when a little
fighter pilot
hit me on a strafing
run.

I also got a sunburn.

here at the end
weary and whimsical
it all
just
fits into place
the world will
always and always
rain shit on you
irregardless
of whether or not
there's a new woman
or an old woman
if the continents are
sliding or exploding,
or if the colors
that define everything
mix together in
some miracle of
transduction.

here at the end
it occurs to me that
bird shit
is actually
some kind of indication
that I should be
looking up.
of course, one naturally
opens themselves up
to the distant possibility of

getting shit in their mouth
but who knows
maybe we all
already
have shit in our mouths
if so, it would just be
more of the same
but if
some prescription of fate
instructed you to
direct skyward
it would almost seem
most incorrect
to ignore the harbinger and
stare resolutely into
the dormant soil
with wings
like that.

Big Sky, big egos

here I am
there I was
this bus is empty
aside from one man
finally coming around the bend
there is a rage somewhere near
taking my head
leading away down
a two foot path
only reconciled with a bottle
just as lonely

and begging to be emptied
as I am
and I feel two eyes
two thighs
two dimples
minds aligned
ripping away
yet sowed
in such a way as to produce
a life as fruitful
as an apple tree
shaking underneath the quaking
grounded wires
and slipping
through a crack in time
I wish I could redo, have back
take with my own hands
and remold
into something that would, could
and should make her smile.

Instead
I let demons, entrenched
rattle their spears, encircle
till I was cowed and chained
a serfdom of shift to bar
close to the opening
of tired eyes ready to work again
just to continue
just to push on
into a black yet blank unknown
in which the end is just
the last time I lose you.

But as Big said
fuck that.

I will build an empire

I will dominate the countryside
sowing love atop fear
and demanding tribute.
"Sam, this is the same thing..."
and I will sit atop the tower
legs dangling
hand in hand
with the newly crowned queen
of everything
we will become
this time
this time
this time
"... we talked about last night..."
is ticking yet
I will not run, rather
I will stand tall and let the bullets
cross my body
as if badly aimed
and my smile
"...I'm gonna go..."
my irreversible knowledge
and your hand in mine
will push oceans
mountains
and valleys
into their rightful place
"..."
as if set there
"...don't call me."
by a hand worth holding.

4:30 AM on Sunday

I haven't slept
since
and its been a while.

these dreams
of cavorting and
dilations
keep me awake
as if they weren't
fantasy.

no rest for the damned
I see.

if only
if only
if only there
was
some
kind of
psalm or injection
chord or manifesto
placation or apportioned subjectivity
to ail
such a vindictive apportionment.

too bad
whiskey
works for
such short periods of time
we could have really been something
this bottle
and i.

you know,

how it is
I assume.
waking up
into a tenancy of
stagnation
one must hold
some kind of hope
for the dictation
of new tenants.

hope is for the
beleagured idealists.

the same
always has and
always will
but you
already knew this

right?

the question is
not
what to do
but rather
what to do
next
but
when next becomes
a tenuous strain
on the sinews and gray matter
and
the dreams that
play to a captive
audience
blossom in full
view of the
despised despondency

thriving inside
said gray matter
sleep becomes a memory
memories become dreams
and dreams keep
me awake

for such

        short

periods

        of time.

                        <u>every day</u>

the good lord doesn't provide for
the misshapen heads that
happen unto the ground.
we are without a
granted code of ethics,
morality,
sanctity.
our spirituality is derived
solely from the environment
checkered like gravel
brusquely astride our
checkered cheekbones.

to us forlorn
heretics
the world consists of the same
molecular basis that
has always been.
the air we breath, the pens we
desperately grab
the string vibrating on the
expansive fret board of our
culture,
all are made of atoms and
power that has
never been born, and
never will die.
when we pass, out bodies are simply
transformed into earth, or air,
or food, so that this
rudimentary fabric can continue
to exist in an interesting
fashion. nothing more.
the meaning of life lies in
the personal ability to
comprehend that we were never
meant to comprehend,
never meant to have the
mental capabilities of explaining
our own existence.
and so we have no god.
we are left behind as
the chosen ones ascend into a
heaven of misery on earth,
while we laugh and sigh,
abused and confused,
as heathens.
we know that
the good lord doesn't provide for
the misshapen lives that

happen according to the
reality apparent in our senses.

and there's nothing we can do.
i for one,
raise a beer, staring at the screen
with a contemptuous scowl,
a sneer,
a soft smile,
and an understanding forgiveness
rolled into eyes that are tired
of a lack of cohesiveness,
drinking deeply.

i'm going to bed,
the small death,
to forget and remember,
all over again,
tomorrow.

Oct 12th, 2012

The air is crisp and cold tonight
offering no barrier or any semblance
of resistance to the merriment
of the normal voices
carrying over
from the porch across
the expansive driveway
here and there a cicada still chirps
although the incoming frost
has driven most of the rest to ground

maybe the remaining stalwarts
are just as stubborn as the cigarette
limply hanging
from my outstretched hands
or maybe it is the dim flood lighting
meekly stretching over
the brick expanse of porch
below my feet
that simply gives the impression of such.
Either way, they seem to be the only voices
aside from my own
that I listen to with any intensity
these tumbling days.

And here I stand, charred lungs still expanding
and contracting
a pulpy heart beating right alongside
and muscles still clinging to the remnants of the finished
glass of wine standing ever so resolutely in the corner
here I stand alone, just as I started 10, 15, 24 years ago
finally figuring out
just what it means
to be me.

To be human.

So what if I do, how the woman
I so adamantly can't remove
from my plane of existence,
said
got a little girl in me.
So what if I am the proverbial nice guy.
So what if I do travel the road that so many
yet so few
have traveled immediately prior to me
in the grand scheme of things.

It is all just the great bandstand; the tiny little speck of

atoms on a flake of dust floating through the
primordial stew of emptiness.

It is just one man's journey as a being via an
illusory transience that somehow gives grip and meaning
to the nothingness of time and space.
So what if I am who I am.
In 100 years no one will know my name, nonetheless
remember
just what it was that I was or wasn't.

All that matters is that I can type and breath
and smoke and listen
to the last cicadas on a cold brick porch in
my sandals with an empty glass
of cheap, sour wine as I
finally figure out just who I am amidst a tumbling,
swirling random chaos
in which the only thing
that is seeming to matter is
that for the first time,
I am content with everything about it.

Fuck this blank page.

sophie

she was beautiful
airtight in the classical sense
her name was Sophie
like my guitar
I thought
at first
that she was an honest
whore
down on the Bayou
so I took off after her
right down bourbon
me drunk
her high
she rolling down the street on a
classic board
me hot footing it
trying to help
she didnt need it
I gave her some advice
she didnt heed it
so we took the streetcar
and talked some more
my stomach rolling
my mind not processing
what should have been shame
her face just beaming
I got her to smile
big
more than once
and still blinking
I tried to get her home
come hang out
but no
her advice
on where to go

held strong in my mind
and she rolled on
just another pretty blonde
headed toward destruction
just like all of us
out those squeaky, thin framed doors
vomiting on the inside
and I remembered who I was
and I finally
finally
finally
went to sleep.

one fried egg

i've been over powered
tangled as if bound
and fleshed into a sense
of humility so profound and
sensical it seems
like a tapering brand of courage
that lingers on my dry tongue
like ash.
the bed is in the sea around me
rolling with the gentle swells
and the walls contract and
expand as wards of the
pale blue sky
that shines blue
if your head is high enough
to see
and all I need is a periscope

as
i'm rolled and molded into
a fetal ball on the sheets
till morning, pacing through
the mental motions like
socks in the dryer,
and hoping to knock off and
wake up sane.

little voices

I hear voices
distinguished and imaginary
although if I were pressed
to determine whether or
I might just be caught
between a rock and a compromise
skipped
across the face of the water
as we're arguing about weather
and whether or not
we were simply
bitching or explaining.

I can hear their tone and auto
-matically assume that its negative
and automatically assume
that its about me and auto
-matically it is suddenly playing
into the realized version
of the realized version
of everything I hate about myself

potentially being
in the eyes of a father
I dont know
yet whom
somehow
I became
automatically
in our conjoined
absences.

These voices are imaginary
a Knex set, a pile of Lincoln logs
the basket of which is held by a brain
stubbornly determined to switch
to biodiesel
to make everything grand and spectacular
into the ash-coated, post-apocalyptic
reality b-reel
that allows for multiple persons
to inhabit the same oblong sphere
all of them screaming and hollering
for attention
for admiration
for purpose
for some goddamn peace and quiet
for.
And they always seem
to get quieter as
I get louder.

professional

she was child's play
a gleaming grin
two notepads
and the loose fitting
frayed hem
jeans of a teacher
I actually could
might have
liked her
it it all weren't broken
crushed and pulped
her face was round
back lit cherry red
across dark mahogany panels
some brewery
deep in the bowels of Bogota
and she would smile
she would laugh
we would
and darling, I really
tried
she was, you were
sweet and charming
we left to that
ever so famous
hole in the road
aguardiente and Pokers
ante-ing up on a
jet boat to tomorrows hangover
"i wish you were
staying longer."
as if I had
never heard that
as if I ever had
enough time

to try
to try
so she smiled
and said she had
to get up early
as my body caved
exhausted
ready to turn a page
but her smile curled
and waved off the back
of the departing and soon
to be torpedoed catamaran
luring me toward
bait
and I was hungry
so I left her
standing there
on yet another corner
in another Capitolio
promising to call
alluding to stay
and ultimately
lying to know
I would never
step foot
on that corner again
walking away instead
giant burger in hand
blue legs
one cold, ashy lump astride
bleating lungs
and an old song echoing
through the marble
hallways of my mind:

"you are my sunshine..."

"...skies are gray..."

"... please don't take my sunshine..."

Child's play.

"...away."

even the losers

she smiles at me and kisses the air
around her face
she's beautiful and i'm in the mood
for beautiful things
so I saunter over and
pour two
three
four
shots of some girly flavored vodka
she's clutching like a shotgun
in the apocalypse
I try for a while to
get her alone
but eventually resort to
cruder tactics.
she bends over to grab her
fallen phone and
I squeeze her ass.
she giggles and pours
two more.

an hour later i'm laying naked
in a pile of arms and silk sheets

lazily smoking a cigarette and
ignoring the pillow talk
she says she's free in the mornings
if I ever have the time
her hand hasn't left my junk
but she says
you don't have to stay
naturally
I finish my cigarette and put my pants
back on.
she hands me my glasses and smiles
kissing the air around my face.
as I leave her room i'm overcome
with potency
and
I can't help but think,
why can't these things happen
a little more
regularly
as I step back into
the party.

duh

for once I cease to be hapless
this fire-laden enema of personality
has rid my soul of the catastrophic
lynch pin that
for ages
has trembled at the slightest touch
ready to spring out and
snap.

misery can consume even the most
tacit and irrevocable elements
of resistance
and it loves company
it takes a realization above the
routine of a drab monotony
the reckless plunge into the
abyssal plain extending
from the shore.
I had to see the inevitable
consequence of an
inevitable condemnation.
I had to see myself presently
in hindsight.

only the self can chain itself
forbidding an immersion into the
foreign arena scathing internally
and twisting out onto the
cutting board of rationale.
this is a process, a learning experience.
you can take it
run and never
ever
look back
or you can sit in your seat
immobilized in an irrational terror
festering internally
tacit and complacent with self-loathing.

isn't the answer,
as if there could be such a thing,
obvious?

shuteye

The stress has a way of gnawing
through the pulsing mess of your
bones straight into your heart
and beyond into a phantasmagorical
wonderland of space and energy
all culminating in a general disposition
of caring way too goddamn much
about something that is way
too goddamn pointless.

Like termites boring into the wheels
of a cardboard rickshaw
I feel the foundations shiver
jittering along with the legs supporting
a frame askew and caterwauled
in the utter ecstasy of impending doom;
of the last release signalling the fall,
of that time when you sleep dreaming
of sky, of terminal velocity,
of passing that imaginary line where
the bell goes off
the fifth round, the 4th quarter
the start and end of a day
wondering whether it was worth it.

Your arms shake in a tremulous ecstasy
pretending as if they were strong enough
to carry the weight of everything you put
on your own shoulders, a magical
mystery tour
of crock, of jettisoned aspirations
gone lofty goals, gone shooting
blanks in the vacuum
just another future astronaut
swallowed by the pragmatism inherent

in alcoholism and those idealistic fantasies
usually reserved for the closet.

Like the famous argument
the chicken or the egg
I cannot determine just what came first
the anxious determination or the resolute
steadfastness of waking up every damn
afternoon with my dick tearing through
my shorts, my ears pinned back,
my shoes already tied
together
those pants you've worn six days in a row
caught up in their own holes and the
previously snoring man
catatonic in his own panicked reveries
just waiting for a respite as
the alarm warbles
just seconds away from
forgetting to go off.

residual heat

it's 8 o' clock and I sit here
alone in a windowed kennel
missing pieces and counting minutes.
you tell me my
writing
draws in your breath, cracking sharply
like the ice blistering inside of your coffee.

I say that

I look like Charlie Brown,
not Snoop,
too focused on, of all things,
myself.
Emotions that I
can't put my fingers on,
run my program
into the ground.
Excuse me for laughing,
honestly.
Excuse me.

It seems that everything we do,
we a constructive form of me,
is in the interests of an altruistic wonderland
designed,
for all intents and purposes,
to make everybody as happy as possible.
With every child left behind.
I figure that I, the splinter cell
of a prototypical lunacy,
should hold myself up as a
simultaneous example of what
not to say, and what not to
leave unheeded and dripping with
sarcasm like
rain, outside the window.

cynicism is a much,
much
better way of describing it.
when the sun is shining
I am outside, laying in the
green blades on the lawn,
running barefoot and arguing
with the bulging sky,
pregnant with the heat of
summer.

it is only when it rains that I,
we,
come inside to write on
our
tattered notebooks.

white Cadillac

my dad used
to have a white Cadillac,
one of the
boxy old models
with the cross jutting off
the front like a carved woman
sculpted to the front of
a yacht
supposedly to ward away
storms. superstitions never
hold true
anyway
we would drive
just drive
away from my mother
his mother, his wife
the women
the dirt and grime
the world so full
of people implying
of people trying to keep me
from forgiving this monster.

I would ask him all of the questions
I never got to ask
like why the traffic lights always
change
or why on rainy days
people always walk faster.
"because they aren't wet yet." he said
only now
do I know
exactly what he meant.

I remember feeling invincible sitting
on the polished red leather
crisp as the day it was bought
thanks to the miracle of neuroticism.
he would stop the car and
spy some girl walking nearby.
oh! he would yell as he rolled down
the window,
"marry me!" he would scream as
I tucked down, chuckling.

he would show up at school
on this white stallion, businesslike
in his suit, yet
childlike with a pint of ice cream in his hand.
my school got used to my frequent
dentist appointments.
he called it 'springing me'.
I knew it was beating traffic, still
the ice cream was easier than
math
and the moments cruised
along down Barbur, Boone's Ferry
and the north shore
before the six packs
and the yelling
the thrown anythings

moments in time where
everything resembled normal
and nothing mattered outside
of the crisp confines
inside a vehicle
made less for driving
and more for forgetting
everything that drove us
away.

from my sky mansion

so here we are
how to start
how to begin the endless
those pointless meanderings of mind and antimatter
rattling around the pale globe
hovering above the shattered and shivering fingers
the walls of this dive bombing cafe
cannot help but hope to contain

so here we go
down this dead end road
the balled up paper a familiar yet foreign face
percolating under the accumulated dust and grime
from so many trails, gas stations, hotel and living rooms
and, of course
the chaff of pale skin and hair being shaved
from dying
like zest from the rind
at such a pace as to literally take your breath away,
one small, hovering flake at a time.

Here it is.
A house of cards gone house of mirrors.
Stitches and sutures gone scabs and scars.
Minutes gone hours
and those irrelevant catastrofucks of circumstance
gone humdrummity, frivolity and pedantry.

Here it is. That realization that you once pretended to have a
dream,
when really, all you wanted was the space to breath
a pretty girlfriend
and the respect and adoration of a cadre of chums,
and now that you are in this caffeine haven
you realize you have none of it,
as you have run away from
every
single
thing
that made you who you are.

It's this moment where you realize
that every conceivable eventuality
and actualized formality of justification
has fallen off
like hubcaps around that one potholed corner
littered with the carcasses of human spears and shields.
And the reasons that you are alive, alone and constantly losing
lie solely in the actions of a man
who is simply maladjusted
bad at life
if you will
put it so bluntly.

Here you go, my friend, have another organic fig newton,
drink more of the coffee you can't handle
speed down the road to another mediocre nowhere
and keep your head above the water

somehow merciful enough to stay
just shallow, enough!
not to drown in.

The water is rising, friend, the coffee is percolating
methheads are pacing back and forth
outside of ratty hotel rooms
one of which
I will own soon
for a night
my mom wants my shit out of her basement
and the go-bag of essentials is decaying and starting
to smell like roadkill, despite how minty and
refreshing
the toothpaste stuck to the bottom might be.

I can't help but look around, imaging the lives
of this upper-crust dandruff
giving them inauspicious beginnings and
inspiring tales
that serve to distract a mind
a ghost
driving a bag of bones
of stardust
waiting for the woman and the man
one of whom should be mine, the other
a friend
both of who know
they are fucking one another
while I know
that they know and they don't know
that I know and the days goes on
round this cafe outside
of the city adjacent
to the crumbling hotel, the springboard
of a life cast, albeit just for now,
among the shadows and antimatter
of time resolute

so here we are, here you go
drink up
this road goes on
and, despite the curtains drawing
to a close
intermission at this overblown
watering hole is over
and it's time
to act
as if it was all
everything you'd always wanted.

blues

these have been hard times
as we make them to be
as the song goes
if only, one could strum through
till the tongue brought answers
melodic epiphanies
how many times do you
need to watch the gnarled and
knotted back of
someone scratching and clawing
as if those two
pairs of words
meant something discriminate,
definite, definable.

this life, this subjective reality
that calls home these ravages of minds

is not welcoming for the likes of those
that question its bounds.
we are mortal, we are fallible and
we, without exception, are going to
die. we live in a flicker
the time it takes a candle to be
snuffed out
by an avalanche.
as such, I should take no heed into
the judgment that steeps you
in boiling water, only to cool down and
have you drunk.

its easiest to kill
indiscriminately.

and
aren't
frivolous objectives secondary to
a greater enlightenment?
I guess that's an
impotent solution
yet
these things we know
that are calibrated towards
such advanced society
amount to a blank check for a rapidly
degrading foundation
yet, in the grace of our infinite knowledge
we stumble
and these somber notes ring through a guitar
emitting sine waves and
rhythm
rocking your chest
back and forth;
a weeping willow caught
in the laziest of breezes.

And for some reason, you feel better,
and suddenly,
it happens again,
one more time,
one more lost thought,
one more song,
one more day.

that time of the month

these minutes don't mean anything
my teeth hurt, chattering and dancing
like a wind-up toy.
my rent check bounces and
suddenly
im failing
suddenly
despite the comma
i'm a failure
slack to be pulled in
a perpetrator.
I've been sold out by a bank
to itself
for money.
what kind of irony is it
that must be told in such a
manner as to humiliate
disappoint.

I'm supposedly on my own.
Missing work
late on bills

talking to myself.
There is no help offered and
no help on the way.
The wrinkles on my forehead are
starting
to crease, oiled from sweat
till red spots bulge and
sprout white infestations
an infection breeding its way into
the front of my skull.

I'm only worthless if I want to be
but sometimes
mainly right now
I can certainly see the
light
in that conclusion.
I can see the weight in
that conclusion.
I can see the pretty little
red lines
surrounding the letters
of that conclusion.
A friendly notion.

I'm getting another beer.

love this hate this love this hate this love this hate this love
this hate this love this hate this love this hate this love this
hate this love this hate this love this hate this love this hate
this love this hate this love this

I don't know why it hits so hard
it's just how I am
my brother says it's chemical
that I don't have enough dopamine
that would explain the cigarettes
but I
can't decide whether to
play a victim or a more
causal role

i'm talking to an empty room
as if my words
the echo of which rebounds against
the planes and corners
like thousands of tiny
rubber balls
are as worthless as
I fear they all are

what happened to the ignorance
that covers you for
too little time,
I wish bliss was attainable as
a calculator
a stepping stair
a shoestring
to hang from.

meditation is for the peaceful
some of us need to throw
shit against the wall
my mind works as a double
edged sword, cutting into the
closest estimation and the pre-
fabricated constituent
reality brings the hardest mind to a
dull point, which leaves
only breeds of insanity in

the mutating mindset.
what is left but the monsters
I turn my back to?

as a matter of course
of course
you could
just as easily
find out who you want to be
in stark contrast to
what you actually are.

but
would you
the stolid manifestation of the
fingers of Mephistopheles
in real time
leave the light on?

or would you just hide
unflappably stoic
in saying, directly
to my face
that I wouldn't
that I could never
possibly
in
a
million
years
even conceivably

understand.

Smashley

her face was a permanent cherubic smile
and her laugh made the branches clap
slowly
as if they were amused.
She seduced me, as she says,
although some lines catch fish
just waiting to get the hell out of cold water,
just like some poems elicit words
waiting to burn through a nascent turned ancient
foolishness
that she smiles at.

I tried to run, just as I will again tomorrow,
and got as far as two broken legs and two crumbling knees
would carry, supporting a frame that just barely made it
to this space, this place, this bodice
of wildflowers turned paintbrushes
and wild beasts turned traffic jams.

As the sun rises and sets, till it doesn't,
it will always be the same, till it isn't
and hearts left closed and jaded
will be inadvertently pried open,
left gaping with millions of molecular gashes,
as window panes toward what we never wanted,
till we did.

And still I will try to run,
trying to reattach the spike to the papermache
canyon walls
as I scribble chaff onto notebooks
in the hopes that it will throw
them
off the scent, all the while knowing
that I will turn around at the slightest hesitation

to reconstitute exactly what it was
I came for in the first place.

I'm 16. Good luck.

You know
those friends are a cancer to
whatever kind of soul
you pretend you have.
All they know is to smile
big white flashy
teeth paid for by doting parents
or haggardly grandmothers
with equally flashy, pearls
of teeth and wisdom.
They know to smile because
they've seen what makes you tick.
One night of drinking and
they've figured you out,
you've told them the stories.
Hard not to.
Against all better judgment
you trust a pair of eyes and a
flapping mouth that waits
till you're weakest
then spits venom
into the deepest recesses of your heart
where it boils until the blood
is black and your nails are falling out and
the wall is torn and broken and dying and there's just not any
air anymore

and you wake up wanting to kill
and go to sleep wanting to
nothing ever changes and the dreams
nightmares really
they come and come and come and come
and never stop and the days become dreams
nightmares really
of waiting for something different, something else
something to spur hope in your brain to
neutralize the acidic content of
flesh, bone and water
in which the sharks swim and churn
tearing at any loose bits that
you've casually thrown off,
casually forgotten, casually untied
till its frantic and you're ripping at your ears, your hair
your thighs trying to find the self-destruct button
for a blissful release, for a calming implosion
for a burger and a goddamn milkshake before
the chair.

The fins are the worst
as you can see them coming,
they make triangle trails through the surf as they approach,
their eyes cold as death and wanting more more more more
more more
and it never stops until
i'm leaving
nd my shit is out the door at 3 am
and i'm the crazy one, i'm the asshole
i'm the shit-head loser who couldn't hack it,
as if this blatant lack of any shred of humanity, this complete
and utter disregard for anything even half-brained
is.

sever me important

upturned noses
fake laughs, annoying British accents
whispers
clueless bartenders
who don't like English
palm frond ceilings
and the imminent foreboding
that inevitably comes with
thick dark clouds
covering the moon
all smoothed down below
the smile necessitated
by three days later
no IVs
no frat boy doctors
gone nurses
no sweltering backwater beach towns
and certainly no fucks given
aside
from: where to next?
how can I jump off of that?
and where is the next
English written book
I can disappear in?

let them come, let them talk
let them live their judgments out
through an amortized
Karmic Payment Plan
my eye is opening
and I certainly think
that I might just be
able to detach from
reality enough
to finally, actually

live.

Scranton

I remember the fall breeze the best, especially the way it pushed through my organs as if stirring a thick stew. I could see the trees glazed across the rolling hills, an amber and canary yellow sea of decaying leaves spreading across so-called 'mountains' in the background. Every couple of seconds a browned and forgotten carcass rolled across our feet, just millimeters apart, toward a final resting place in the roughshod gravel. Her cheeks were slightly pink. Every time they angled up to mine you could see the faintest hint of glimmer on her bones. She was irritated about something, I could tell. Her lips were cold. We were at the mall, an apt place to spend our last hours together I guess, standing outside above the train yard. Next door was a national monument recognizing the importance of these metallic caterpillars. Strange place.

I had traveled out to this barren corner of the U.S. map just to see her. Just to smell her again. I had stayed up for two days straight, my hands shaking, waiting. To see her surprised smile. To pick her up and spin her. To feel her shuddering beside and underneath. How could I have known we would spend the entire time fighting each other. Fighting ourselves. How could I have known that I was the worst kind of fool. The fool kind of worse. Now here we stood, resolutely in love despite the obvious failings of our constitutions. The rusting trains beneath us trembled in the cold just like the bums that had no doubt stood inside their decrepit frames, huddled around flaming trash cans like Icarus around the sun. We had forty-five minutes till I left. The trains just stood there and watched; I swear I could hear them laughing.

The irony was fucking palpable.

An old friend once told me that the only ones you remember are the ones who you don't follow. He called us 'star-crossed lovers', all just caught up in the game of trying to smile. All just caught up in the game of getting up in the morning.

Every time I try to tell myself that I hate this woman, that she was just a waste of time, I just think of her face with the trains stacked behind her. My mind goes blank, unfeeling, numb. My eyes glaze and suddenly I'm there again, forty-five minutes till I need to go, our feet just millimeters apart, her lips as cold as the breeze churning my stomach. The train yard laughing with iron lips. The yearning of a prolonged adolescence. At a glance. I can't help but smile.

Somebody let those stars fly.

Choo choo, motherfuckers. Time to take a ride.

one more and the tab

they started a poetry reading
spontaneously
and the snapping starts
and here comes 'the understanding'
that these pea coat toting socialites so crave
that lasting impression of wellbeing that somehow
corresponds perfectly to the cadence of words jutting
from the 'PA' via the mouth of some whitebread
cookie
rocking back and forth beneath a baseball hat
with a flat bill
and straightjacketed between a v neck t-shirt

what isn't to admire

the conversation lulls before it even began
and the crowd oohs and aahs with each memorized
blasphemy of rhymed words, every catatonic
capitulation to a false reality in which that which
make us human is more than just the sweating pores
of our rapidly dying skin
they actually believe in hope and love and romance
just words, fleeting words, that seem to drift in and out
through the cracks in the wall

theirs' is a misinterpreted reality
spawned from a white, middle class
dreamland in which there are no succubi
gutting the juicy
hearts of peaches
beating tremulously in their death throes amongst a
toxic canvas
there are no whores or bums or thieves
there are no souls hungry for any of those things
that allow people the luxury of dreaming;
of imaging such an arrogant fantasy for themselves
there are no children forced to eat their rusting spoons
as the dog sniffs at their swollen bellies as if timing the
right moment
no impossibly long nights spent in the cold
as brutal as the glances cast
by the cookies 'mingling' in front of syrupy sirens, muted
in the futile attempt at projection;
at trying to hop that fucking moon.

call me a pessimist if you will.
call me a hypocrit.
call me a pizza.
you still make me sick.
to me, the true nature of life involves taking in the entire
breadth of
that which makes a block a clock, a syringe an escape ladder,

a set of words a parachute and a serated knife dripping the
foulest of oils.
Utah Shane once told me, across an impressive moustache
and
a lukewarm beer, that the key is to laugh
as the whore tramped across the gangway and the fools
paid for their malice with sugarplums seeping from their
pee holes

yes, life is beautiful.
but the roses are all covered in shit and to ignore that
is to make yourself simply a product
of the Glee club, the Twilight era
the fucking Britney Spears soundtrack to This American Life.

so
keep your rosy colored rhymes
the polyphonic spree of syllables
those bliss drizzled utopia cakes
and your manicured hair
away from a dank hole made for hiding
let those of us
caught up in the trenchant realities
drink whiskey and laugh away
troubles made by you
and your Dad
stop fucking snapping
fawning, idealizing
grab her by the ass and
straight to the back seat
for all i care
and get expediently to hell
anywhere
you want
as long as it is
out of my goddamn bar.

Unchecked Rhetoric

The day rolled by as if it was nothing
just minutes cast and reeled back in
against a tumultuous current chalk full
of driftwood and dead fish.
Despite the amazing view afforded by the
traversals of hillsides and minor miracles
the sunshine peeps through the clouds
for mere moments before the minutes and
seconds remove such gleaming vestibules
of hope from the lofty heights of mind.
It's as if we're all doomed to live the life that
we don't know we're living till it's
too late.

How did it ever come to this, we ask,
how did the end of the road come so suddenly,
with so little warning?
Did I really achieve so little?

The words cast on pages and across intermediate
expanses of water and air are simply the resonance
of chords that we do not heed, that taper off into
an infinite chaos with such definite relative proportions.
The thoughts and ideas that define us waste away
in cells made for nothing more than the passing of genes;
the production of more minutes and seconds.

How did it all go so wrong?
Where did I make the fatal error?
HOW DID I FORGET TO RECORD THE DEBATES!?!?!?

...what do I do next?

10 bucks says he won't do it

the bug is unstoppable
chomping on my nuts as if they were
gobstoppers in an arctic ice storm,
rattling my nervous system till my
brain is incapable of anything short
of complete compliance to ideas
left autonomous.
my hands are Uzis hovering over keys and
my heart is a typewriter methodically
pushing pages upwards to a throat that
can't vibrate for lack of any kind of purpose.
creatures that I regularly fight in my dreams
emerge in front of my eyes as if challenging me
to slay them with the mightiest of pens,
with MIND BULLETS, with the only thing at my
disposal: the brainwaves melting the words
onto the pages that swiftly move down the screen
never to see the light of morning, eyes worth entering
or any kind of paper left unwadded and unthrown into
spit smeared trash cans.
still the bug gnaws and gnaws, eating what it will
of my poor testicles (but what have we DONE!?!)
in an effort to spur something great out of
something not entirely sure it is capable of some
thing of that magnitude, or even the definition of
any of the descriptive words and adjectives used
to describe any of the sentences used either to
write this down or describe anything close to
that nature.
and here I've gone losing myself in the verse,
in the snap, crackle, pop of my virility exploding and
the crackling of papers being rolled into cancerous
treatments that will inevitably need
far more cancerous treatments

simply because one man
can't listen to his own
nuts.

Balls.

sing a song for me

The street was getting dark and my socks were getting wet so
I leaned over and set the guitar against the wall. On my right a
mattress lay limply crumpled on the floor beneath the weight
of a thin blanket, a thinner hat, three or four shreds of paper
and now, a 32 year old blonde who knew my name. I think. On
my left, an original Star Wars IV: The New Hope poster, sepia-
toned from sun-stains and a life of smirking with impetuous
confidence. In between was an oppressive stench and two
murky-red eyes loosely focused on the narrow divider of air
and space. I couldn't think of the line I needed. Wouldn't come
to me. I had been working on the song for a month, almost as
long as it had been since the first time I saw Her. I'd been
playing the same chords over and over to the street four
floors beneath me, pushing grainy words through the gap in
my face. As if exhaling could sum it up. I think it was from a
fictitious Italian mobster that I learned the concept of the
'thunderbolt'. In his case it hit him at the sight of a barely legal
minx who ended up getting car-bombed. Mine was simply the
street artist who always set up outside my window on the
bustling street below. I liked my odds. My tiny apartment
shook with every broken chord, every off-tune note and every
snapped string.

"I had something to tell you..."

My poor fish, already irritated with their recent food selection, were forming a 3D version of two beautiful women, one Japanese and the other what appeared to be a mid-20's Serbian, vociferously putting their thumbs downwards in disapproval. Clever bastards. Quick lesson: fish will try to eat anything if they're hungry enough, except yogurt. Now you know. The woman was snoring loudly, something that has never ceased to amaze me about women. Aside from the fact that they fart out of their pussies after a good fuck, they *purr* as they sleep, little lioness-vixens with the vibrational profile of a sub woofer. No wonder they sleep naked. It's a good time to say that I've always realized that it's a little odd to be conversing with my fish, especially considering how much *practice* it takes on their end, but that's life. Sometimes your fish disapprove and make sure to tell you so. Now you know.

"...but I can't remember what,"

The rain picked up, as often happens in this city, bombarding my windowsill/shelf/desk as if it was just another American citizen in a northeastern African country. In the distance a helicopter resolutely chugged its way across the high rises like a predator drone. Thinking about how expensive those windshield wipers must be, I saluted the sky outside the window, stretching every inch of my frame straight in the air. I puffed out a chest, bony from negligence, in a salute to the patriotism of our environment itself. Truly a land of the free. Fight Terror. I snapped the rest of the bowl.

"...I had something to show you..."

I first saw her in October on the last day of sunshine. It was noon on a Tuesday and I was recovering from time travel. All that was left of my armor was a red hand print spreading across my face, leftover breakfast and a beer soaked wife-beater. I vaguely remember smiling. I had looked over to my right and seen the girl's purse lying on the rumpled mattress.

Shit. She was going to be back. I looked out the window. The new She was in a canary yellow dress, an impressively droopy sunhat, and had paint all over her hands. Her easel was aimed down the street along the street car line with the sun pinned onto the sky in between a smattering of slouching towers. Below the easel was a bright green stool covered in small bowls of paint which she would alternately dip her brushes and fingers into. I sat transfixed, watching the bottom of her dress whip around and around as she danced and painted. Danced and painted.

"...don't think it'll make the cut..."

A flash of inspiration surged through my brain, immediately pulsing through my blood stream and counteracting the poison seeping out from my sinews and synapses. I grabbed the nearest sharpie and began to write. Dressing quickly, my eyes turned to the fish. They were forming the words: "My sources say no". Insolent little pricks. When I bought the damn things I figured I was getting a low maintenance pet, not a cynical peanut gallery. Fish are just like women, you see, you buy them for their appearance then you're stuck with them for their legal rights to sue you for negligence. Now I know. I left the door open and flew down the stairs, a fresh white piece of paper gripped tightly in my good hand. Let her break anything she wants. Hopefully she'll have mercy for the guitar.

"...so from the very bottom of my mind..."

I remember the door slamming behind me and the frosty cool breeze of Fall sweeping through the street. The air, sky, leaves and acres of cement all carried the same reddish-orange tint; the color of a tragic death perpetuated in the grandest of comedies. She was standing in front of her easel with her hands on her hips, the tightly bound yellow curb of her right hip jutting upward in contemplation. Leaves fluttered across the ground and teased the hem of her dress. As I crossed the street, she looked up. "Shit." I thought. Hook, line, sinker. I walked past her easel to the telephone pole a few feet away and tacked up a piece of paper that read: "You're beautiful. – Sam, 4E" When I turned around she was staring at me with a thoughtful expression across her face. I immediately choked, lit up a cigarette and disappeared around the corner.

"...just stop and look up,"

"..."

"..."

The woman began to move in her sleep. I'd forgotten she had the tattoo across the small of her back. I'd also forgotten her name. I wondered what I'd told her my name was. It was then that I saw her walking, a closed umbrella in her hands and that same droopy hat smeared across her head. She walked by often. Every time she did I tried to play a little bit louder, a little bit better. I picked up the guitar and tried it again. I could never see if she looked up because of the hat. I was also too busy thinking of the last line. That elusive last second slam dunk that was trapped between the world and my window pane.

Son of a bitch.

"...and I'll open up these blinds."

Not a hard decision for most.

Two options remain:

One is to fold and whimper as if cast
under a bus by brutally callous hands,
a reaction that is clearly not your fault,
crying out for mommy and the alluring
promise of decisions not made and
opportunities not followed as if possessed
by a demon spurring the greatest effort
imaginable in such a glorious human
frame.
The other is to behave in a manner that
benefits the entire community around
you in an attempt to make the world
a much better place for all, despite
the self-inflicted detriments and grime
one immediately finds one's self mired in
up to the tits, irons resolutely cast around
each protruding follicle of misplaced arm pit
hair coursing from the pathetic human
frame.
Once a man understands this dichotomy of
himself he begins to realize the inherent
decisions that come with every breath; with
every step after another; with every timorous
word uttered blithely into the aether. Upon
this realization a man must choose.
Will you become the man that underwrites the
existences of his fellow men at the expense
of the copper toned moon?
Or will you become the man that breathes the
air as a living, breathing facet of the overarching
goals of mankind: to finally break out
of the crushing confines of this withering
frame?

Momentary lapses of murkiness

Moments of clarity come in searing flashes
as if the greasy, faux-shag carpets weren't just soft as pillows
or the ancient apartment you sit in atop a hat store isn't
creaking
isn't swaying at the beck and call of mild breezes
or as if you can't hear every single voice from the bar down
the street
booming through the alley.

Suddenly it's been three weeks since you wrote anything at
all.
The rain still comes down, the chalk mudsliding through the
indented cracks
arrogantly flooding through as thick pastel pink, blue and
green caterpillars
towards drains choked with pine needles and rotting cigarette
butts.
Yesterday the sun was eagerly trying to break through cloud
cover thick as wookie pubic hair;
we were all just those tiny figurines fixed to the bottom of a
snowglobe in a microwave
turned to extra-low.
Suddenly these details mean something to me.

This was all just supposed to be one big training mission. One
huge endeavor
with the grandiose purpose of gaining, gleaning and garnering
a voice to write with
when the whole time it was simply a self-sabotaging, myopic
railroad track
holding a cannonballed and rusting train car filled to bursting
with one battered occupant,
rolling across a wasteland spattered
very generously

with moments of startling narcissism.

Suddenly this wasn't who you were supposed to be
just another man caught up in the grinding transmission of a
mid-90's car left in idle
sprinting from table to table with baskets of fries
standing on a porch bathing in the aftershave of rain, cigarette
smoke and burial mounds of regret
poised for the next spring that fails, every time, to finally close
the hatch to the cellar
with one finger left loosely caressing the flimsy latch to the
door outside.

They think you're stupid.

So make them see, oh brave and tenacious mumbler of truth.
Demonstrate just why it is that health care isn't just an
economic boon but rather a moral prerogative
tantamount to the greatest undertaking in the timeless
battlefront of social, political and economic equality;
just why it is that we strive to get up in the morning and smile.
Every single day that we have.
Illustrate that while global security is a reality-based
necessity it is not necessary to sacrifice
everything
that we hold dear about those ethical imperatives that such an
illustrious protagonist as Jesus
found it very important to expound, at length, about why we
should just fucking do it.
Show them that cancer can be beaten just as acne can be
beaten just as polio and smallpox can be beaten
the same way we defy gravity with every short flight to
Denver for a 5k and some new breweries.

Take these evident truths and hold them dear, but take away
from the preaching long enough
to make sure your boxers are facing the right way. And your
fly is done up. All the way.

Suddenly it's not just a headlong dash but rather a brisk yet
leisurely jog through city streets
overflowing with those who strongly believe, those who will
buy into the game plan.

And then the moment is gone, they weren't listening anyway
realities bend with each emptied glass
we are nothing but that which we consume
and right back to the cautious optimism you go
ducking and dodging, peaking over the trenches you've dug
waiting for bullets to graze your head and maybe, just maybe
one lucky enough to take you out faster than emphysema
or that plane to Denver fireballing at 500 miles per hour
and this carpet is comfy
so comfy
just one 18 by 12 bed sheet
taking in my face and arms as it all fades back into normalcy
you're still gone
and these not muted passions
fade
and the words taper
to the screen.

San Juan

Here we go again
made another mistake
another trip sidelong to nowhere
told them all it was over
see ya
i'll catch you on the other side
and found myself tired

alone yet popular
killed in the sense that I had
to sell myself
to be myself
and something for them that
they've never seen before
yet at the same time
have I
so here I am
writing about myself in the country
Hunter S
made his own
the idol I always wanted but
never thought I deserved
and here I am filling up a page
with nonsense
wrapped up in everything
that made me run from ghosts
goddammit I am more than this and I always
will be
everything that I will ever free write in a foreign
country i've always dreamed of
yet couldn't make happen
in the sense
that I didn't plan for
what was coming
only what was going
past outside, scattered as trash
and no wherewithal to go back
half to shame
somewhat in relief
choking on the sounds of my own voice
just ready ready ready to capitulate
to that which makes this
absolutely bearable.

here and there

Lost, lost, lost again
just watching tattered bags drift across the street
I dont even know how long its been
since the only thing
ive wanted all day is a release
just another scattering of rain and leaves
blowing across a parking lot I want to call home
even though theres no solace
in yellow lines and tumbleweeds
and I fucked it all up again
and its taken me months
just to wrap my head around
just
how
shitty
I
can be
they say that the first step to recovery
is accepting you have a problem
but I knew I had a problem and put her in the car
kissed her
and said goodbye
and then I had a whole lot
of other
problems
I don't know how many of them I
can
accept
there were so many nights I didn't care
as I gave up in that hole
in NoPo
as if that ceiling fan, that dog ridden couch
could fill the hole that I dug out of myself
with a homemade wooden spoon

as if I could drink
a river of tears, liquor
and the promise that insanity lies
in believing it will all be
different
this time.
My mother doesn't look at me the same way anymore.
Nobody does.

It's missing, as if there was ever anything there,
feels like theres a piece of the bookshelf gone foundation
that was torn out
cracked and sliding down into a maw of loathing
never to return
as if something slowly died while holding my hand
and crying really, really fucking softly
teardrops running quickly over
the map of disillusioned time constructs.

What if I did sell everything worth selling
and gave away everything worth giving
took off on a jet plane
that immediately felt wrong
to an island of man and welter
riding taxis and drinking cheap beer
as if that was the life
as if
that could float a lost soul
sinking through to the trenches, reefs
and chumming fish
soulless
in their pursuit of something to tear apart
with teeth meant for swallowing whole
as if that
was exactly what I did.

That island took one look at me
and I gazed back

nonchalantly
and resolutely at times
just another drifter
caught meekly wondering
what the next step should have been
as he boarded plane after plane
toppled mattress after mattress
and eventually finding
himself
high amongst mountains
where the hell
am
I
this time
covered in a glistening, pale
white snow
lost, lost, lost
like,
top ramen with sriracha two times
a day
and boat shoes
in four feet of snow
lost
just staring
nonchalantly and resolutely
at tattered bags caught against the side of the street
and leaves buried and rotting in piles
under mounds
of those yellow lines, picket fences, parking lots
and the dreams, ideals and misappropriated homes
that pushed me into
here
drift as snowbanks
ramifying into pseudo-glaciers
chalking their way through
the confluence
of everything you thought you'd find
on an island, canyon, mountain, beach

far away from what you
thought
you'd be
somehow there
somehow where
you find yourself now
lost and finding
you're
not
as bad
as they
thought
and there's so much time left
to be lost
searching
rescuing
and
of course
releasing.

to the wall

now it's a truck stop
gambling room
drinking a beer
I can't taste
that I shouldn't be
not tasting
inside are muffled voices
sighs
and dead looking bouncers

outside is Easter
cracked yellow paint
and an empty bus stop.

She's in tears now
of course
and I am considering
highly
laying down
on the curb
calling it in
one last favor
from the pavement
once so cruel to my oh my
such a dented skull.

Now its an empty town
caught in the Montana 70's
chock full of memories
just an overgrown asphalt grater
catching the blood dripping
from broken knuckles
poor door
and she challenges me
telling me to let go
and the choir sings
in the back of an empty
room left unplugged

please just let the minutes
pass faster
let my eyebrows grow monumental
exponential
to hide these eyes glistening
and irradiating
shame, fear and
cemental loathing.

<u>up and away</u>

As far away
as I can seem to get
the images of home
parse through the mug
the palms, the ocean breeze
scything through decisively
into the porridge slowly seeping down
my spinal cord.

I've found, as one can only find,
that the intangible strivances
toward a raw, splintered enlightenment
are nothings
but an organic stop gap with gigantism;
a mental kudzu imploding out onto
the helplessly gentle rolling hills
and lymph nodes
dotting the countryside.

Just stepping out the doors
is tantamount to a day job
you spend hours on.
The mold soldiers on, outrunning
you to the flank and you
are suddenly seared onto an Earl Grey
panzer, rolling across
a trench laid out
ever so gently
across the unimpeding landscape.

And I still become farther from home
as if such a thing was imaginable
with boots on the ground.
Still the scent of oncoming rain

elicits the type of response
one would expect
from a recently returned
thought-to-be-deceased
ramblin' man:
a plateau smile, dulled yet twinkling eyes
and the understanding
that what once was
will never be again
that the battlefield of aging youth
requires grimly optimistic strategies
and that
atop it all
lies the blissfully catatonic
lightness of simply letting
it all
just
go.

"p.s. it's still funny."

with the thunderous heartbeats and
limbs flung haphazardly
coiled and still vibrating
comes the memory of that
petulant coma i like to call
my time with you.
standing atop quickly cooking
eggs splashed with peppers
and hearing the churning of sheets
from the other room
your childish face resurfaces

in the steam rising from my morning
coffee; an impotent, feckless memory
that evokes nothing but the hollow
understandings that come from a standoff
with the tepid realities we all
grow accustomed to
in one way or another.
from these raspy whispers come the
infallible laughter
self-directed yet deprecating in
all directions like a grenade let fly
between the sheets

sounds familiar.

the truth always finds a way to get to where
you can't sleep.
and they wonder why i'm so perky
in the mornings.
still, for so long the currents churning through my mind
were the unmistakable derivations
of nothing expounded upon
in such brilliant displays of Newtonian physics;
of everything you made sure I knew
you hated about me.

sounds familiar.

so what if it took a while figuring it all out.
blasting aside those walls
I so carefully constructed with nothing
but the glare of my teeth and the hair
of my awesome. fucking. goatee.
has been an exercise in ignorance.
the good kind. the rattling of keys being the
only clue as to where the entrance
to my solipsistic paradise and
coincidentally

the only chance
anyone has of ever finding me
again. as if these bare feet didn't need
anymore barbs, needles dug needlessly deep
into the sole, pools of fire from which to
churn the spray of embers falling onto the faces
of those silly enough to follow.

as if these walls needed any more erection.

the steam rises into a gap-toothed smile
and the eggs turn that shade of yellowish-brown
like the teeth of a crack head lost in the bushes
outside walmart,
and suddenly, the memory of you is erased
in a flurry of forks, hot sauce and
crawling back under the sheets
to pull the pin again.

drinking from the host

Girls, they're just girls
they giggle, gaggle and goggle
flitting from man to man as if
they were kelp riding atop a lazy current
underneath a boardwalk.

The one I let follow me now is Taiwanese;
a special blend of naive, raw and conservative
to the point where each giggle is unreadable
as if she has invented a way of laughing
as interminable as her characters.

Every man in the restaurant eye fucks her constantly,
a fact that I can attest to myself,
and she behaves accordingly, bucking and chirping
in 5-9 time.
Whether this is teasing or only the
frivolous meanderings of a child I cannot say.
Whether this is an inscrutable landscape of
windblown shit is readily apparent.

Still I take her to four-course dinners.
I learn her language.
I smile when she says "I love you."

Sill I dance along the line of her eyelids
as if toeing a strip of tape amidst flashing
red and blue lights.

Dating such a girl is fraught with some kind of
benevolent sadism that I have trouble bringing into
the type of focus her countless photos take.
A good teacher knows when to poke and prod,
and also when to withdraw.
Perhaps the best lesson is how to see the world
clearly through rosy sunglasses.
When to fuck, run, reshuffle and gun the engine.

And not necessarily in that order.

#1648

Stuck between being anywhere

and being somewhere so beautiful
I cant define
the list goes on and the hourglass
grows empty
yet still I remain
fully breathable.

Still I remain
retained.

If someone were to have told me
that this would be my life and game
I would have laughed,
then tentatively, when
they weren't looking,
done the same damn thing.

Whoops.

The trivial meanderings of the everyday
can consume such options
better than the beer in my trunk.

And still I blow it with
half the pretty blondes,
every time.

At some point this glass house
needs to shatter to the ground
in a cascade of jagged flakes and drops,
if only to open a window
and catch a slight breeze toward
some kind of flat horizon
with an edge to drop off.

The sun here rises as the trees set
and still, the river flows under the bridge
inside my room,

and still, I do not snap the chains
and

haggling

After the sweat, the piercing elbows,
the wild fracas of drug-addled toys
moving rhythmically, silver sheen coyly reflecting
the brilliant cascade of cerulean blues, royal purples,
bloodshot reds,
and any number of chromatic cues.
After the roaring surf of sound, blasting upon
the narrow inlet of membrane separating brains
from the chaos of air encroaching upon
immediacy.
After the wax and wane, the peaks and valleys,
the pulsing veins and throats nearly ripped apart
by the tremors shifting aside the ridges of thick tissue.
After the skirts, panty lines, lascivious glances,
after the curiously strong clutch of a floor mopped
in spent sugars, preservatives and yeast,
after the sky has fallen and the remaining air,
compacted with each untamed purr and growl,
has shattered into a swarmy blanket of sticky satisfaction,
you cautiously slip into the tenacious dribble,
cool, collected, calming finger tips blindly seeking
your arm hairs like starving moles burrowing to the buried
cheese.

She's standing there, blond hair hanging limply
from her tortured scalp, beaming a death knell
in a finely mustered grace, framing a face
made beautiful
by centuries of vain appropriation.
In her hand she holds a crumpled dollar bill,
the wrinkled facade of the unnecessary;
the curtailed; Plan B.

"A cigarette for a dollar?" She purrs, mews.

Or does she roar? You can hardly hear anyway.
Pausing, you pull out your pack, already dwindling
after a day spent waiting, breathing, gnawing, callusing.
You hand her one of your last life rafts, a burning log
drifting to the naked tendency toward a rain-slicked rock face
of engulfed solitude, a smile haphazardly nailed to
your mask.
She tries to shove the ticket, the lie, the subterranean tunnel
into your gnarled fingers, an equally haphazard grin
blossoming between the small furrows of dimples
dotted onto her face, as if an afterthought.

"Keep it." The low, unused tone prickling the curiosity
of some of the lesser visible hairs on her body.

"How about for two?" The same grin. The same
pert dimples hanging daintily over pert tits.
The drizzle comes down and down.
Goddamn you, orbs of furiously rocking glory.
Goddamn you, helmeted knight of preordained valor.

"Nop..." You start to say, before she cuts you off,
moving close in one swift movement, the dimples
flushing with a bright pink reminiscent of freshly bloomed
cherry blossoms.
You can see the glistening knoll of her lips, almost
imperceptibly rolling back into the incisors attempting
to burrow into her tongue. You can see the tiny pools
of water clinging to her nose, her soft hair, her smooth
scythes of eyelashes.
You can see, almost hear, her breath accelerate.

"How 'bout for a kiss?" She purrs, this time lightly,
so as not to pique the ringing ears of the waves, throngs,
the toys milling around your bodies.
Suddenly you are in her mouth, an adventurous tongue
finding hers in a swirling embrace, tentative and fleeting
yet as soft and warm as the incipient fuzz dotting the outside

of a ripe, freshly plucked peach in summertime.
As your tongue swims so does your brain, spinning
on an axis of greased steel, a perfectly
calibrated gyroscope.

You pull away.
You know why.
That smile. Those dimples. Those tits.
The rain.
You smile. She smiles.
You light her cigarette.

You walk away.

As the night closes around you, enveloping the shards
of your soul and weaving you into an insistently vibrating
matrix of apparent spheres,
it all
you all
of all
to all
could all
for all
what all
makes sense of the puzzle for a moment.

And the rain reminds you again.

lost in prayer

Good god.
What a phrase, just two

words of antipathy, antiquity,
reaping an obstinate blasphemy
the likes of which the world hasn't seen
since Crowley.

What a crock.

Here lies Sam. Rest in malfeasance.
Rest in carefully calibrated cannibalism.
Rest in the ability to finally shut the fuck
down and listen to the world settle
for just the moment.

As if when I die the worms
that will shit out my corpse
are merely angels doing my
dirty laundry.
As if 21 grams is enough weight
to burden my shoulders
with the reigns
of a class too limp-wristed
to take the plow
on my days off.

Don't worry, Bud'.
I will teach them how to love
as opposed to hating
as soon as I get around to stopping
the self-loathing, self-hating
elements of myself.
If you feel like lifting a finger
when I decide to sire you
all the better.

In words and fear
we decide to create the safety net;
the bungee cord so we can plummet
through an existence we cannot comprehend.

In God we simultaneously derive
our own awareness as a dichotomy;
we are both the rulers and the ruled.

If there is such a God then there can be
many more.
Almost seven billion, if one decides to be
ethnocentric about it.

So good Me.

It's so expansively
simple.

aim for the center

another job
another grimy, dimly lit dorm room
captured by the transience of
two feet fluttering amongst
the gravelly sunshine
filtering in through the window.

I have lived a long time, now.
I have waited for the words to come, as
Charles once claimed,
yet these places do not engender
any types of ideas worth
jotting down
past the humbling realities present
in watching the traversal of time and energy
underneath your nose.

That and all of those fat goddamn tourists.

The holes appear in the wall under
the fluttering wings of moths
struggling to have just one mad dash
into the center of the sun.
I envy them.
For such a creature it is so easy to dissolve,
to give into the crushing weight of gravity.
To perish in a fiery blaze of glory,
in the simple pursuit of The Light.

Too bad this will be my last night here.

I could have really learned something
from these insects.

Somedays
there's one
brief moment
in the ol' daily routine
where you realize
that you're totally fucked
asunder like swiss cheese
and left furtively bubbling
in an alligator infested hot tub.

It may
very well
be why they serve
booze in the morning.

peek-a-fucking-boo-hoo

In and out
but not like the burgers and fries
'cause i'm stuck with
the thunderous heart
the catatonic vibrations
of words left uttering
the pangs of regret
left remonstrating.

You'll never see me
stop smoldering.

You'll never see me for long
enough to see
the smoke
anyway.

The realizations inherent
in a good long look
lead to the guise of seeming
permanence
under the pretense
of staying with you.

Of escaping you.

Now you see me,
now you don't.

Now you don't.

preoccupado

The expectation is great
hanging in the air
a cumbersome chandelier
at waist level
and I toy with it
poking and prodding
the silence
as if shepherding
the ghostly stigmas
across the aisle
nipping at the milling
heels of intolerance
meaningless words
and the occasional
amused smile.

She looks at me with hazel eyes
hair dyed bleach blond
the putty makeup covering
her face no doubt
worth more
than my existence.
She wants me to talk.
To validate her presence.

I refuse.

The noxious scent
swiftly creeping
from her neck, wrists and Italian leather
handbag
has already enveloped
the palace guard of my nostrils.
Her nails, cherry red

of course
are clicking
tap, tap, tap
like the clopping
of plastic shoes
down, down, down,
to the 12th step of Hell.

Her shades have glitter on them.

As I look out the window
she is politely harrumphing
and clearing her throat
trying in vain to signal an attention
that is focused
on the rolling, tumbling
hills of Northern California
and matters
infinitely
more consequential
to a means of existence.

And as the ride wears
on, on, on
she stares at me
I stare out the window
having the best conversation
of the day
with the swiftly passing
scene
outside the window.

bed bugs

I wake up to your face
getting fucked in the mirror
as I bang on glass
from the other side,
the one that slides downwards
in a never ending reel
of shame.

My life is better without her
but the insidious roots
of hubris
and whatever the hell I used
to love in that silly little girl
have been tough to find,
nevertheless eradicate.

Such roots bury deep
as I sleep, giving no mercy
to a mind tenuously gripping
the razor-sharp edge
of the canyon
like a safety line.
Still these feet move
forward
dragging a reluctant mind
alongside, oftentimes
saturated with tears
and tantrums;
oftentimes imbued
with enough whiskey to kill
a Brahma Bull in it's prime;
oftentimes accompanied
by a new set
of legs, tits, pussy and ass,

to assuage the marinating
brain, that shattered lump
of gray matter
processing all of these
so-called
dreams.

It's almost as if
I never woke up at all.

re-ashing the past

The smoke makes my eyes red, a fact that can be hardly
noticed in the dim lighting of the equally dim hotel room. How
I got here I cannot begin to piece together using the puzzle of
a ramshackled mind and a duct-taped means of inference, yet
the reasons for being here are staunchly embedded. This
world never ceases to create the journey and meaning
necessary for the continuity of existence while simultaneously
deriving the mind of the means of comprehending the
vastness of such experience. Thanks, dude. I crack a beer.

Here I sit, watching the first game of the NBA season, with the
last vestige of my childhood friends occupying the other
double bed in this temporary household. This abode is as far
as it gets from home, almost to the southeast corner of this
country in a straight line from the colder and somewhat
wetter northwest from where we originally hail. I've driven
across that stretch and more, beginning a journey into the
unknown from which I hope I never will return. I haven't seen
a familiar face since well before I left, yet somehow this held

no weight in my mind till I met my friend here. Suddenly the tide of memory and reminiscence has washed through my nerves and veins, draining my system of the free-radicals of anonymity and replacing them with a somewhat understandable recognition of the outside world. As we tell stories of our current and past lives, rehashing the past while reconciling it with the future, the truth begins to make itself readily apparent. We are no longer the children we once were just a short time ago. We are no longer the people we used to be, although, somehow, we are exactly the people we used to be. If only life was so simple.

The game drones on and on, sports talk peppering the tentative probings into one another's lives. I can tell he is gauging me, trying to determine how much I have progressed from the anxiety-infused, emotionally-driven lunatic of yesteryear. I am simultaneously gauging him, trying to determine how far he has come with his sobriety and whether or not this will last, as well as in what form it will take. It is a stark reality, contrived, if at all, by the playful undertones of nostalgia and the understanding that from the fact that good times were once had, so will they be had again. And the smoke wafts up from the butts ablaze in the blissful aplomb of combustion. I find myself wanting to apologize for talking so much, for I had been alone for so long, yet suddenly find no reason. I am not the weak, eager-to-please creature I once was. My first thought is that I will somehow drive my friend away, whichever course I take. My second thought is that, despite how I deeply appreciate the few friends remaining to me, I simply do not care. I have a feeling that he understands this, although he probably does not see the scope and spectrum of it, and appreciates it as a welcome change. I know I do.

He tells me about his life and I am proud and pleased. Where once I would have been slightly jealous of a friend's success, I now know that their path is not mine and that their successes are thus not mine to judge or compare to. They are simply those people who have accompanied me, in various stages and states of mind, through portions of my journey. I cannot help but encourage the satisfaction emboldening my questioning. I find, through his discourse, that he has become a man in his own right. His choices seem more adult than they used to be. I hope mine sound the same. His stories are hilarious and his tragedies are short-lived and quickly gotten over. He misses home yet understands not only why he had to leave but also, why he will not be going back for some time. We suddenly understand each other. The smoke brushes the side of our cheeks and turns them ruddy, pausing in front of our faces as we laugh and scooting away to unblock our vision of the game going on in front of us.

And just as soon as it began, the evening is over. The cigars are ashed on the side table and he is standing to leave. We slap hands and make plans for the next day, although I am sure that I will not see him for some time. Deep in both of our understandings is the knowledge that our journeys must be undertaken alone, and the continued comradeship breaking up the monotony of deep and continued loneliness only serves to weaken one's resolve. We both have our own decisions to make and we have both gone too far to turn back now, despite the obvious pitfalls and shortcomings inherent in such decisions. Such is life, and such is being a man. I say goodbye to my friend as he leaves, closing the door behind me. I stand up, walk to the mirror and look straight into that face. I passed a test. Whether it was my own or of the world's I cannot tell. Nor can I tell what the object of such a test was in the first place. What I can tell is that while my journey continues without my old friends and the other old companions, I am now aware that I am not alone. I watch the last wisps of cigar smoke trail through the cracked window and smile. Such is life, just smoke passing from the roll, to the lips, to the lungs, to the air and finally, into the ever present and all-encompassing air.

It might just be that easy.

pile it on

I wish my bowels were golden
fixed pipes operating under peak capacity
churning out miraculous wonders
of stench and release.
the shit that is emblematic
of the human condition
is a daily routine that
cannot be missed with any
regularity, despite the misgivings
of the body.

it's the best part of the day,
making homage to the porcelain
white throne, a polished domain
ensconced in pearly wainscoting.
as the minutes tick to hours and
the fan bellows,
i lose myself amongst instinctual
necessities and perfunctory gestures.

if only the inefficiencies would
coalesce into one enormous
body of work.
if only this was more and more
like a confident belch of habit
then I would be a true component of
something etched into experience,
created through ritual,
birthed from an odoriferous sentence
delineating dark patterns
misshapen forms and
a swirling reminder that this has been
aptly done
by so many before.

it could be my diet.
it could be my loins, pushing forward into
the stubborn curvature.
it could be too much booze and coffee.
however it lies, the fact remains the same,
as I will sit waiting and chanting the
rhythmic mantra
of
here I sit
broken hearted,
came to shit,
and ran out of paper.

social anxiety

how did walking become
the hardest thing I do
just the mundane stroll
between two places
that only serve to keep
me alive
for a little longer, without
progressing. Any further
and I will certainly lose
track of why I need
to come back at all

as this crosses the street
I look up and one of these
insolent fucks
is peering or leering

jeering or fearing
and otherwise making
this whole living business
that much
more enjoyable

can't we all just drink our
beer from the can?

it's sunny and I don't own
shades so you can all see
drooped eyes and a dance with
sun beams that you
judge judge judge and
laugh but there is
a shovel dug deep
and it is nothing you
you you can pull out

The Sword in the Stone is a
myth, applicable only as
a metaphorical means
of giving your brain an enema.
which is what sunbeams
do to mine.

these sidewalks get longer as
you get closer, closer
to a subjective wonderland
those closed doors and cracked
window panes that flutter with
every beat laid
palms-up on the glass.

the street crosses again and
there is another one with a
fat spawn grub, snotting and
laughing as she frantically

rubs a rag over his face.
she's a leerer and
I still have no shades.

the music dies in the post office,
the cute girl in
line
behind me is dating someone
who doesn't exist and the
goddamn sun is in my eyes
I want to scream
BURN motherfucker! BURN!
right in my eyes
and I am back on the sidewalk
near vomiting and drained
slipping a little, slopping a little
wanting the sweet release
of mediocrity
anonymity
and a life lived
trapped between intro and extro
ripping and rending
this face apart.

<u>baby steps</u>

I've held her as she sobs
and felt no better,
wishing she would leave me
a hapless whale

beached on a bristling crag
jutting from the surf
either as irony
or just as
ourselves
I'd die for you, she says.
You're more important, she says.
I love you, she says.

She doesn't.

But it will be alright.
I'll be her Styrofoam lighthouse.
I'll wash her dishes,
take out her trash.
I'll run errands and bring home
beer after work.
I'll pretend that we know
each other and vivaciously
tenaciously
tell her the goings on of my day
and pretend that she's listening.

I'll
because I can't afford to leave.
Regardless,
your company seems to
have accepted it's own
monstrous qualities
captivating elements
of the fearless human drama
we wittingly threw
our best feet forward
into
with a splash
worth 10
words or more
and that seems to be enough

for me
for now.

<u>yes, I saw you</u>

she was small like a candy bar
and her insides were the sweetest
ambrosia I might ever find.
she asked me why I always looked
so tired
and the words, those traitorous friends
they ran off, leaving me to stutter and
stammer out silly falsehoods
rather than tell her that
after a fifteen hour day
I found it impossible to lay
just lay
and not take every minute to the second
to not watch the gentle hummock of her
shoulder rise and fall with every one
of my baited breaths
to not tell her that it was for these moments
that I got up in the morning to
do it again.

oftentimes we would sleep
angry, frustrated and content
in the knowledge that
in the coldest part
I would clutch her delicates
and the warmth
would return in a explosive
exposition, erasing
all worries, all tendencies
all regrets of tomorrow.

Another
girl
called me Sam Sam

yesterday. I had
to put on my pants
leave
shatter my phone in half
and set, fist on chin
holding back tears and apologies
till I could
reconcile
a thought with a stare
with the idea
that something had always been
missing before you
fell through the laundry chute
with the lies I insistently
told myself.

now, the day is cold and bright
my eyes are still tired
and the minutes chug by like a
grotesque apparition
left to welter in the heat
of existence, so far from the
bliss of purgatory.

it's been a longer while
now
I still
wake up clutching air
memories are the currency
to a starved mind
images in the mirror are closer
than they appear
I am a rich man
till my feet hit the padded turf
and my eyes droop downwards
in the knowledge that
the new one
isn't you, isn't that

everything
isn't this supposed to be
just a goddamn vacation of
remembering
what it's like to be a young student
of life
love and
happiness
and to already
have lost everything worth
working for.

Jim

my eyes don't want to cry
but my heart is having none of that shit
and my hands don't want to type
but my head is far too lost to not
sow seeds in little, irregular black lines
and where the fuck is my typewriter
and where the fuck is my pride
my uncle drank himself to death
this morning
as if no one saw it coming
as if he wasn't already as alone as
he was going to get
running out of family at a furious pace
running out of shades crushed beneath
pummeling feet
and against my better judgment

I still love these people
and I should really just let them die
but I think of their smiles, their goddamn
adorable
little country quirks, this is the blood
that runs in my veins despite how
we have collectively forgotten that fact
on a daily basis
for years
but I just think of that poor lonely bastard
alone at the end with only his trusty old friend
that damn bottle of cheap brown whiskey
in the plastic bottle the one that has been
my friend for as long as I care to remember
the one
that's my friend right now.
and his words echo in my mind:
"where's the BEAM at!?"
and his drunken pupils
flash and dart in the darkness
above the screen
and his checkered red cheeks stare at me
in the mirror
and the time he let it slur that he's
glad he had a son who could
drink with him
and the time that I had the notion
that I had a Dad
who'd talk to me.
and the time I never told him that.
my uncle drank himself
to death this morning,
just a race to beat his mom,
and now i'm here in buttfuck Utah with
a ticket and no itinerary
a bottle and no friends
worth mentioning
my girlfriend is getting fucked

and my eyes don't want to cry
but my life is having none of that
and my hands don't want to type
but the whiskey is having
no more of that
and we are all men,
we all die,
and I let him die
and I never told him that.

Same shit, different life

After long enough
you can talk about anything.
After long enough
you have the innate ability
to recover;
to recollect the marbles
from the chalky gray
grass spattered circle.
You suddenly regain
the voice
that was strangled
by the barnacle encrusted
claws of your lungs,
an insatiable pearl made of tar
rolling in time
to a tenacious heartbeat.
Like waking up as you fall
out a door 30,000 feet in the air,
you scream
in grim satisfaction

in solipsistic ecstasy
knowing full well
the universe is about
to End.
The ground becomes a manageable heap.
You become larger
than horizons left stretching
to snapping
like yoga pants between broken hands.

You land.
You smile.
And you save
so that you can
someday
take off again.

looking up

son of a bitch
quit bleeding and seeping the foulest of pusses
just stop and let me
catch my breath for a minute
this is my life and I've chosen
to obsess about the most
of the interesting
and the flashes of sky
I can see as I roll head over healing
down the side of the mountain
breath breath breath
get up
I will not give up, give in

s for one second to let
you
catch me
but goddamn you fucking cocksucking
son of a bitch
stop tossing unnecessary hurdles
under my stumbling feet
just let me keep my
distance
dust let me sink my teeth
into the wolf I am chasing
I am thirsty
my teeth are white and yellow
and crave the crimson
as if iron deprived
just let me go for the jugular without
sending these little bugs to
devour my cells from the inside
out.

<u>transparent</u>

And so it begins
the next molecular free fall
the next traversal across a plain
f existence I didn't know existed.
Mr. Sanborn, you're on
in 5 minutes...
Where are your pants!?!

Strap on my boots, the faded leather
reminiscent of the aged faces of

the ghosts that blindly wave
as I pass through.
The pack lashed to my back is heavy
with gear, process,
lashes and lessons learned and
the ever present anticipation
of anything else, anywhere.

If I live till today I will no doubt
laugh and cry with the punches,
surfing the harbor of this swaying train car
as if caught in the swells
left by massive behemoths plowing through
oceans made lakes; behemoths I will
one day be.
One day; one gritty, sweat soaked sprint; one foot
in front of the other
till they are all blind as I am and
lost in plain sight.

easily guessable title

You can wake up 1000 times
and still see their faces
turned to the side as if sneezing
out the scent of your now
anxious pore popping.
These mornings aren't fresh white
pages; they're pendulum swings
bracing for the come back
but you're still covered in newspapers
balled up pieces of whispered words
and the mercy blanket
she threw over you before she left;

before the sun came up.
Now they're laughing and applauding
as the hero rises from the splintered
boards
CRACK
and so it begins.
Just another sprint toward the inevitable
realization that it *was* that simple.
I just failed to
make it that way.
Watch this man wake up 1000 times
and make a bold dash to the sneakers
which he will use to run as far away
as he can
from the light that hounds him like packs of dogs
Licking at his ankles and screaming
WAKE THE FUCK UP SANBORN.
As his knees collapse and bend underneath him
and the breath drains,
leaving him panting in anaerobic bliss
without thought, just the mind numbing
aches of muscles left to snap, tendons
already gone and the resolute bones
left to splinter onto the floor
enveloping the horizon
above and screaming

WAKE THE FUCK UP, SANBORN.

WAKE THE FUCK UP.

another crazy drifter

Sitting in the dark in my car
my home
drinking a pint of nice whiskey
and talking to myself
devising imaginary conversations with
imaginary people
speaking of topics I would
never speak of with
normals
in a tone I would never use with
normals
wishing that I had some kind of
company whatsoever yet
still relishing the opportunities
inherent in being alone.

Somehow I am in Maine.
That sentence reverberates as if
I am a tuning fork and the very notion
of spatial presence
is one big flick of two big fingers.
This is not
normal.

Tomorrow I start work but frankly
dear
I just don't give a damn.
I know that I will have to sow and
plow to ply myself to
continue eating
but right now the whiskey halting
that tinny reverberation has corrupted me from the
roots upward.

As I piss I hear the demons and ghouls
approaching at a rapid pace, my heart
quickens despite the obvious realities.
There are vampires behind the log
that want to eat me.
There are zombies making their way
across the woods to devour
my gray matter.
There are cancers flashing across my brain
like lightning strikes, threatening
to knock out the entire grid.
Zeus' famished wrath.

My car is rolling
as an immediately located tectonic plate
has decided that I am too heavy.

This is all
really happening.

I am still talking to myself.

Someone once said, somewhere
that it's your own fault
if you're lonely.
If that is true, then it also must be true
that it is your own fault
if you don't give a damn.
Well,
whose fault is it if you have both
noble traits
tumbling around in the ol' dusty dryer?

Either way, I believe
these fermented tears
are helping.
Yet my red plastic cup is no longer brimming.
It is sagging.

And there are only so many molecules
of water and salt
left in this storm-torn host
that I am such a parasite to.

I just wish I had somebody
normally worse
to talk to.

And maybe another bottle.

Gripping the back of a seat
as if clutching a loaf of bread
swaying to the tide pushing
back and forth in time to
the gently, sloping, twisting
contours that follow the coast
like a wounded dog
trying, not diligently,
to keep my weight off
of the German angel smiling
out a sand-coated window,
a thin beam of sand-coated sunshine
peeping in through sunflower yellow rags
passing as curtains.

We're all just passing through,
passing out, passing downfield,
passing away. Yet a smile
remains the only immortal timepiece,

two canines and two gold pieces
gracing grimy faces as if beckoning death
to come relax
and have a beer or two.

The minutes tick by unheralded,
unwatched by doting mothers,
neglected in the surf much like
broken sea shells left sinking
into a beach that will, no doubt,
engulf them along with us.

Against my arm rest tentative fingers, bravely
lost in a foreign channel, a sepia-toned memory
passing from eyes to brain,
to mouth, to ears,
to pen,
and back out the exhaust,
crumpling uselessly yet mirthfully
onto yellow squares doing their best
to become lines.

know then

It's hard to believe that the world knows
a bigger fool than I, but maybe
that's just the compliment to a lifetime
spent pretending to fool around.

Short plot lines, ruptured songs
and the breakneck pace of the drummer
rapping furiously on the back of his heart

lead him to believe that the body
is simply the vessel of innumerable
reckless, feckless and hectic musicians
although that might just be the
blame song.

Nevertheless, we find the foolish
protagonist aloft, 32,000 feet in the air
eyes drooped with the strain
of an empty wallet and the pangs
of self-inflicted heart sickness.
While it is the bold and brave
coward who bares his chest and refuses
to shirk away
from the ranting of a pulsing heart,
it is the logical and tactical of us
that close the bleeding sutures early,
who neglect emotion as the unnecessary
ball and chain affixing one's legs
to the illusory ground.

A less foolish man than our ramshackle hero
would have cut the ties long ago,
leaving the sweet taste of angel's breath
to rot and decay on the path behind him,
a foregone conclusion to an otherwise believable
short story.

Instead the awkwardly stoic lynchpin
of said journey
chose to empty said pockets
on a meandering search for said angel,
ultimately doomed, knowingly,
to the slow crush of his heart between
the unsympathetic vise of distance and time,
blood pouring from the sides
like a peach
crushed between the iron grip

of a platinum-hearted villain
consumed by follies
and loathing,
aiding and abetting the drive to such
endeavors of blatant
yet epic
foolishness.

like the fly circling the globe lamp

I'd like to call this
The Fall of Sam
but honestly I can't remember
when I wasn't falling;
when it wasn't all wrong and
I was just another nothing
caught by the neck in a noose
that I tied.

These pity parties last for weeks
in dull shades of gray
and all different sorts of archetypal
caricatures,
almost seeming at times to be
recurrent nightmares written with
the sole purpose of
scaring myself to death.

And the phantoms move across the screen
and I am here alone, dreaming
of a situation in which I could have all
those tenuous trappings of happiness;

those illusory means of conveyance
through an ill-defined aether atop a
bumbling steed.
These things are more than a woman,
a car,
direction.
They are the definitions that we choose
to be delineated by.

They are that which make us unique.

Without them it all appears, and rightly
of course
to be simply a scratchy dream state,
complete with the holy terrors and drunk endeavors
of a Friday life gone very, very
right and wrong
along the way.

fleedom

Kick the tires and scream
a giant standing toe deep in a pool
of last night's stale beer.
Those women foolish enough to cry and care
do just that
and if my head wasn't swimming; if my feet
couldn't slow down their inertia
I'd still be headed right down
the road to nowhere.
Look at me,
I'm a bird, a plane and, quite possibly,

Superman.
Still I sit at some Sysco-worshipping
side road diner,
the overpriced sauce
spilling into the mouth below two slanted eyes
and all I've got left
are way too many empty glasses
a silent phone
and two quietly shaking hands.

devastating relief

"Your heart is beating really fast." she says.

Oh really?

It feels too good. Like the last episode of a sitcom drama, where the tension is finally relieved, she is in my arms. I still hold back a little. I still wait for her to do it. It's just another stunted growth of time and fate; another night spent with the woman of my dreams. The woman who is so much like me that I oftentimes get lost as to what we're talking about, as I don't remember who spoke last. She is my Holy Grail. This is the woman I cannot have.

Here she is giggling nervously at the tribulations of life. Accepting my overtures yet, so fucking gently it destroys any resistance I might have, pushing me away. It has taken me years to wrap my head around it. I have made no progress. Whatsoever. The undulating warmth and a vibration as smooth as goose down I can feel pulsing off of her body echoes through a chest hollow of my own volition. Ineptitude would be a better word, although I am not man enough to admit it. Yet. Cementing the delusion is the childlike bond and understanding that lives would be exchanged without a moments thought. The intimate understanding of everything, despite the fact that I'm never around. The way she knows, yet won't admit, that it's because of her. It's always been because of her.

Because it hurts too damn much.

Here she stands, head buried in my shoulder. In shame, embarrassment or joy I can't tell. I may never understand. It feels as if this has happened a thousand times, although I cannot remember any of the other times I have simply said it. Simply admitted it. It makes you want to believe in a rotating existence of soul and spirits. It makes you want to believe in anything she will tell you; in the archaic adages of love, cupid, Aphrodite and the penultimate strength of the heart. It makes me want to believe in the bottle I know is lying open in the trunk; in the park that I know I will end up in, again. Swinging in the same damn swing, wondering how it would feel to fly for just a minute. Before I broke both of my legs and had to get another bottle.

When I met her she was a train wreck of epic proportions. Whatever she had done this time around had been repaid in kind. Tenfold. I had taken the job over three others because I had seen her behind the counter during my interview. I was fresh out of an office job, applying to be a cook. I could have made 40k a year. I wanted to take a break, to enjoy life. At the time I wanted her. Realistically, I needed her then. But she needed a friend, an ally, someone who wasn't going to fuck her over. She needed me.

So I loved her without needing anything. I kept it close to the cuff. When she kissed me that one night, saying those words that haunted me, I stood and waved, watching her safely into his car.

"I adore you, Sam."

I pushed and prodded toward what she needed to want, and I was always there. Friend was an understatement. I tacitly and directly supported her, checking her mental state to make sure it was balanced, shutting down any kind of evidence of the ruptures cutting through my chest like flak through a B-52.

It sucked.

But she deserved someone in this world who would not let her down.

Tonight, I was selfish. I couldn't keep it in anymore. She is the most beautiful woman in the world. When she is happy, my spirit flies. I cannot imagine a more supreme happiness than watching perhaps the only person you have ever truly loved laugh and smile in an innocence painted in berry juices across the beaming, childish face of the sky, with a complete disregard for any past or future denotations. To simply be, smile stretching the corners of the sun itself. It is the only time I have ever known the supreme satisfaction I'm sure fools must feel when they are sure of something. It's a damn good thing I've never hesitated to be one.

Call me a dreamer.

Now here she stands, her hands around my neck, her soft hair nestled on my neck and her chest pressed strongly against my humming bird of a damn heart. She is giggling and snorting as I tell her that she is the most beautiful woman in the world. That I would take her anywhere. That the choked, muffled words are nothing to me. That I would give it all up. That I would do, well, just about anything.

Except stay.

Seattle Sunshine

sun creeping in through shutters
i thought had always been open the
stark realities become blissfully
realized
it's so simple in hindsight
it's so easy in progression
the trivialities of life are simply
simple again
and anyone can see that

the travels one undergoes with neither
a gas tank or a fat wallet
are those that truly demonstrate just what
you bring to the table.
walking the streets and looking up at the
booming towers the shit stained pillars the
cracked walls gives one the perspective
of roots yet also the understanding that
it takes a climb to
summit the top of the heap.

even those words uttered by those
trying to impress
trying to facilitate something better
at the expense of someone they
will never understand
even those careless actions
perpetuated under the guise of
semblances of reality are naught but
a ticking and tocking off a human
mechanism, a clock left to rust and wither
in the sun as your feet
keep walking.

and the sun comes out.

She tells me she screamed my name
as she came under
someone else.

Sweet.

Now I find myself retracing
footsteps and tracks,
tracing lines on some kind of
grand paint by numbers
kaleidoscope.
These mountains loom invitingly
yet the facts remain the same.
I am somehow still
just following; two steps
behind.

Caught, without
being captured.
Alone, yet surrounded.
Pacified, yet louder
than ever.
Petulantly appropriate
and
screaming to just myself.

sundialed in

there's always the time line
right under your nose
whether or not you believe in it.
While the substance itself may be
a massive, pulsing, wobbling ball
undulating through sentience
like a popped inner tube atop
the murkiest of lakes,
the faces, places, and states remain
part of the infrastructure
building your mind.

As your eyes see, as your ears hear,
as your heart pangs for what you've lost,
the illusory clock mindlessly ticks,
senselessly denoting the progression
of infinite molecules moving from point A
to somewhere I don't care to measure.

Still,
right in front of your nose the air,
the world traverses, the universe abides.
Still,
our stubborn clocks persist.
And still,
the trenchant building blocks
of your memory and mind
persist without changing,
as if they've ceased trying
to fight the clock.

brotherly love

The bastards left me.
Simple as that.

I've tried to live a lifetime
under a code
of my own making,
the first rule of which
is never leave
a friend in need
behind.
My leadership, evidently,
is severely lacking.

At the pits, the bottom, the lowest
of short paragraphs,
the bastards abandoned me
to my own devices, floundering
under a rain cloud of my own making.

What are friends for?

Now, here I sit,
recalling names and hand shakes,
homes and friendly places,
a complacent homeostasis.
Here I sit contemplating
exactly
what went wrong, as if
nothing was wrong in the first place.

The truth is.
I don't blame them.
We all are known

to flee
when the going gets rough.

Who could reasonably
expect any different?

The fact remains,
however,
that their faces remain
lodged in my memory; their personas
etched in my tales.
It's not like a woman, where you
can drown the memories in whiskey,
beer and skank-fluids.

They were my brothers,
and the bastards left me
behind.

Somebody page the captain
as there
are iceburgs ahead
and blood
in the water
and
the lifeboats appear
to be burning
and
there seems to be a recurring pattern
here.

rememorial

oh hi
memories
why don't you
just flood in?
take your time
you won't wipe
your feet
anyway
just kick back
and keep me
from sleeping
this time
that time
again and again
it's ok
have a beer
whistle a tune
as I strum along
just sit there
let me look at you
reanalyze
as if that could
change anything
as if that
could make anything
even remotely better
in the sense of
how it all
panned out
some gold rush
eh memories?
just the same issues
that have come to define

this discourse
and I loved you, her, it
every time
but every empire crumbles
in my case exceedingly
fast
the tides always change
and nothing deemed
worthwhile
ever seems to retain said worth
after a while
so stay a bit
memories
let's pick you apart
and gain acceptance
solace and gratitude
till tears and smiles
pervade the space
once defined
by something altogether
more free
and worth remembering.

lamb stew

You wouldnt recognize me.
It wouldn't be the same, anyhow,
yet I sit and watch the same people
with different names and faces
say the same silly words
trying to humble my self to
such a present of reality.

Remember when I was overly cautious,
when I thought they all
hated me?

Then they can't stand me
but they'd love me
if they gave it a chance
goddamn
I was lonely .

Now I couldn't care less.
Wax on, wax off.
Easy come, easy go.
One way, please.

Passing by the Disney channel tonight,
the television a source of noise more
than any kind of reasonable means
of entertainment,
of a meandering discourse,
of an abatement of
the sickening feeling intermintedly
mixed with the hops
and barley
ever present in my stomach.
Some black singer with sexy little lips
was singing about some kind of love
I will never come close to understanding.

She must have sucked one hell of a dick
for that gig.

All I can think is whether I can remember
the last time a woman gave me those kind of eyes
without hearing the clicking of the engine
in the background, without feeling the blood
start to race outwards towards the very tip

of my fingers and toes.

Without immediately turning my head
and pretending
I didn't see.

I can.

I usually just chalk it up to
not being
in the same place for long enough.

I know better.

You wouldn't recognize me, the
battered face and tattered clothes hanging resolutely
astride the thick glasses and crooked smile
resting atop this well-used hotel mattress.
You wouldn't know the beer-stained wrists,
the smoke-stained eyes.

I hear the kids in the room over cheering as I
pluck a new guitar, trying to work out some
of the more entrenched patterns of misbehavior.
They are easy to ignore but somehow harder
to forgive and forget for things
they never could have imagined that they have done.
As if they had ever existed in the first place.

Yes, this face is new to all but the cracked windshield
and the wheel polished around the brim as if it were
the brass fittings of a candling, floating on a fall breeze
seemingly on it's own,
right by the windows of a well-lit house,
the sounds of a vibrant family dinner
setting sail across the smooth surface
of the passing pressure shift.

But wait, here I sit,
the sounds of a town I cannot remember the name of
streaming through my nostrils like cooked lamb,
becoming something altogether
foreign of recognition.

sloshing in a can

Trains move slow and stop often
like old women picking fruit at road-side markets,
examining each blemish and stain with the acumen
of a diamond appraiser.

Just more time to pretend to sleep;
pretend to dream about things that aren't you.
These mental pictures, fuzzy scriptures,
and huge armfuls of rotting fixtures, seep
through from behind my eyes and ferment,
a controlled bacteria eating into an apartment
I already sold.

C'mon already. Let this train derail like Virginia.
Let these fields free of the oppressing sprinklers,
feeding the needs of these morbidly obtuse passengers,
as I steal the plane in the background
of this idyllic scenery, watching
myself fly away still nailed to the canvas, bloodshot eyes
still blinking
just as the white mosquito crossing the horizon
detonates on the side
of the nearest hospital.

These buttercup yellow fields,
bubbling with camper vans,
subjugated refugees and the general hurry inherent
in the flight of birds from the coming cold,
drown under he fog and smoke,
gurgling incoherently as if
miserly.

Crawl train, crawl.

Beats walking anyway
and why lie,
to pretend I have somewhere to go
would be pretending like I hadn't
drank in a week.

Cheers.

<u>see you next time</u>

From a faded blue seat
I see through the window
of a greyhound churning my guts
away from that sad relic of a town
holding back
in the final vestige of summer.

The last failing grip of the climber
slowly slips into the frigid crevasses
of winter, the leaves seep
their crimson blood onto the panes
of my eyes, deciduous vampires

frothing at the chops
with the syrup of the final kill
of the season
freshly dug from the hesitant ground.

The phone tucked beneath my nuts
chimes and warbles
emulating the flocks high-tailing it South
alongside the highway,
just another woman
throwing consolation
to the winds of breath
of a fool in love.

She asks me
how it looks, but I can't get past
how it seems
and the pastel purples
and pinks
swathed over the front of
these billowing clouds
do nothing but remind me
of her sheets, of her
wine-stained teeth,
of the sweet pink glow
cast between two little lips
that still
reach into the deep
recesses of my mind,
puckered as if sympathetic,
entranced as if mythic,
the dusty trail
illuminated only by
hindsight and the
glaring knowledge
of ne'er do well
and should know
better.

prison management

Even when you know,
even when you just get it,
get everything,
understand the context
and underlying meaning,
this doesn't stop you
from boiling over
the bile bubbling and burbling
up into your throat
like a noxious cauldron left unattended
over a roaring flame.

Suddenly, you're the snake,
fangs sharp and sopped
with a seeping venom
seeming as if to pierce
the air between
you and those foolish enough
to make contact,
spearing their saran wrap facades
and inevitably
terrifying them into leaving.

Stopping the flow
has become a lifelong obsession.
Yet no path of recourse
alters the inevitable result.
Still the fire burns
and burns
and the savage truth remains.
I am dangerous.

This face of yours has been

carefully tempered into one
of niceties and compassion,
leading one to almost believe
that you are
one of those
benevolent souls.

Like me they are
jittery potential.
Like me they are
invariably unalarmed.

Like me they are
fools.

reveling

After falling through the branches
for what seems like a lifetime,
the parachute appears,
dropping from the sky
like sunshine.

Next thing you know, you're floating
toward the ground, a bird's eye view
the only thing covering your ass
from what comes next: The Landing.

As you fall
birds occasionally test your resolve, and your skin,
but you've found a knife and a sharp set of teeth.

Feathers fly.

You've got a pretty good idea of how to handle
the little bastards.

As the wind tears out your hair,
the rock ledges as rocks ledge
barely missing the inevitable shave of karma and leg,
the branches snap in a steady rhythm
and your back becomes the lightning rod
of the aether's bad mood.
You snap into consciousness; into
a moment of sober clarity;
into a euphoric nightmare of
eating, drinking, smiling and jerking off.

The savage blossom above you erupts
again and again and again,
taking such a heinously frail existence
away from the rock face
and letting it gently float toward the opening maw
of the ground below,
a concept so goddamn beautiful
it invokes delirium,
when you don't have to stand on it.

Like a self-conscious satellite
I am the omniscient eyes and ears
of all below.
I am the King of all that is,
will be,
and hasn't been approved
for a second season yet.

A lion is roaring in my ear.

Someday this will all be mine.

Somehow, this will all pass.

So why,
of all things,
does it seem to be
such a familiar
descent?

faulty wiring

There's a switch somewhere
if you can find it
tucked in the back of your brain
lodged like the one chunk of obsidian
in a field of shale
uniformly gray yet somehow gleaming
in a morning meant for walking.
From a chilling damp an oppressive fog
bears malevolently down onto
your bare shoulders.
The crows are laughing,
the crows are cackling.
The ground is mawing
beneath your cracked feet, the bared teeth
a benignly mischievous grin atop a world
of surly. Yet you come strutting through,
swinging shoulders as if such
motion could bear fruit,
or wings.
As if from the cocoon you emerge, dew dripping
like sap down soft bark,
evolved in the imaginative

sense yet the same in all senses of synaptic
patterns, excepting the now burning pilot light,
of course
and you laugh all night.

on the abouts

Despite the best of intentions
often the only thing I can see
are the pitiful subtractions
from that which could be created
in such an idyllic state.

At the middle junction I find
myself tentatively jaded
fed up with a future
I'm not sure will ever exist
due to a present
I'm not sure is occurring.

And they keep telling me
to keep on keeping on
in the present of one's being
and to maintain such maintenance
that keeps the body of work
humming.

It's almost as if the answer
to the riddle is a riddle
in and of itself
and the final answer to
the inherent riddle in

trying to solve such a
riddled riddle of an answer
is so convoluted with
fucking bullshit
that I can't
seem
to
add
it
all
down.

A very pale and hungry Thor

The bolts tear down
as they heal a lonely mind
battered by the currents
and strained
to the point of snapping.

The young man in the cheap hat
strums the guitar blindly
the chords as off-key
as the raspy words sung
just a hair off-beat.

The hoodoos sway
whether to the music
or in discomfort
no one can tell.
The lightning bolts
however

have a lot to say
a fact made abundantly
clear
to the ridge in the background.
If the young man
could only play lightning
rather than just the rain
dampened clay
staining his feet red
he would be Thor
of the Canyon,
Mephistopheles
of the grand vibrations.

He would be electric.

But as he plays
the brown, felt hat
swirling and shimmying
atop the simmering forehead
he knows that he will
either shock himself
or totter home alone.

"C'est la vie," he sings
and the lightning
crashes down.

4.6 trillion

I live at the blue crater
a hole with a penchant for water

the fate we all fall into
as an obvious yet sentient rain.

Let it pour.

As I branch out, rutting and rooting,
the bristling wildflowers erupt over
the parched rock, a gentle wind
twisting their stems
as if twirling golden locks of hair.
With a coy smile
of course.

People do seem to come and go
churning their ass fat
in synchronistic rhythms
just another parade of unknowingly
depraved observers
waving giant foam fingers
they call perspectives
toward a moronic conception
none of us can ever hope
to understand.

And the rocks smile in the bright lights
to the bluest deep of the deepest blue.
The flowers dance in the lonely fields,
beckoning to all of those
brave enough to climb the crags,
all of them silently bellowing
the calmest of pleas:

Why can't we just move along?

current events

In the churning shallows the winged insects lay eggs,
dive-bombing down into the valleys of clear, green ice water
as if unaware of the dangers present underneath every drop.
With each successive dive my admiration increases
for these widowed mothers; these fearless harbingers
of future generations. Their tenacity leaves one wondering
whether there is more you can do to ensure such a timely
delivery of life and continuity. Their twenty-four hour lives
remind one of their own mortality. Their very existence
reminds us of our own.

Imagine that from the time you woke up this morning to
the time that you are now reading this underneath the dim
lights
of a coffee shop or a battered studio apartment that you had
already been born
already frolicked in the childish morning of life
already matured through adolescence
already met your mate
already fucked your brains into oblivion
and already sowed the seeds of a thousand children
that you will never meet.
Suddenly the day becomes that much less of a measurement
doesn't it?
From seconds to minutes to hours to now,
where these intrepid mothers brave the unseen mouths
of hunters below along with the tumbling, tumultuous current
what was once a mere day becomes a lifetime.
What was once a child becomes a mother and soon, a corpse;
a meal; a future.

Unlike the kamikazes of old these bombers populate
the unforgiving expanses with building blocks inside

holes, as opposed to creating them; to leaving
charred wreckage. And while the latter may be
exactly what life is, the fact remains the same:
the widows dive on
the river turns
the sun claps down on the water's edge with enthusiasm
the author scribbles
and hopes
it is all so simple.

                        flying this town
                      feels like the others
                    all just loose associations
                         silly people
                          odd goals
                      intertwined into some
                            thing
                            some
                             one
                    not there from the dawn
                    could possibly recognize
                       so an itch festers
                         feet beneath
                       this last cheap
                        resting table
                   horns blaring, cans flying
                        seconds ticking
                       as I stuff my face

anxiously awaiting departure
to a destination
I don't have.
<u>knives and spoons</u>

It only seemed like a good idea
when I was drunk
lonely, heart shattered
itching.
I snuck into what used to be
my room; our room.
I pulled aside the covers
slipping in my leg
cautiously as ever
as if I was slipping
into a pool of boiling soup.
Her side was soft as feathers
yet unwelcoming.
As of yesterday, her heart
belonged to another
like roadkill being thrown into
the dumpster.

I knew I shouldn't be there.
I knew it was wrong.
I still wanted to do it again.

When she woke she started screaming.
She'd probably been fucked
in the mouth
that night.
Probably thought I was him,
crawling in.
Disappointment is a nasty breakfast,
like toothpaste, orange juice and
rotten bacon.

Good morning.

Now the insults came
from that same hole
I used to put my lips on,
the same lips now contorted
in direct opposition to those
that now harbor the current bottle,
controlled by the mind starting
to contemplate the next
as a very good idea.

So I slide out the door
and hear the lock slam
behind me. As I step out
into the crisp, cool air of Fall
I fight the urge to puke all
of that out.
There might be some booze left
in that ol' stomach of mine.
Either way, I take no chances,
heading straight to my room
to open the next bottle.
I'm late for work, but that's no matter.
I'm riding high.

I love being Big Spoon.

Ernie

Ernie's got the cancer
bad
but he refuses to let himself down

as I drive him to appointments
and for burgers and shakes
he won't eat.
The man known as the Weasel
crawls into the rainbow
shot by a cumming sun
and laughs, laughs, laughs,
directly challenging the fate
of so many before him.
In jean jacket, jeans
and thick, wire-framed glasses
he looks the part of the Marlboro Cowboy
missing his lung;
the part of the stalwart American icon
standing resolutely
against the crushing weight of thunder
and gravity, and the pestilence
eating at his bones.

Ernie refuses to succumb
until he is ready.
He refuses to coalesce.
Ernie may have cancer
but he is not a whiny bitch
like you or I
Ernie has a heart that still beats,
bones that still hold,
arms and fingers that still flex
and he will not
cow to death like a coward.
No, Ernie will serve his contract
the way it was meant to be served:
staunchly. Till the end.
Soon Ernie will be flung into the sky
like a burn out on the flight deck.
I'm driving him, dropping him
off at the hospice center
an odd collection of Asians

half-wits, drunks and travelers
along to watch.
Ernie doesn't care.
I buy him a beer before he goes in
that he won't drink
"You're the last good friend I'll ever make."
and slap his ass as he walks through the door.
He has seen it all and on a warm breeze,
he will see it again.
I, for one, will watch proudly,
knowing all the while that this man
lived life true to himself,
as he dissolves into the sky
perhaps broken
but never beaten.

cut to pieces

this blade is sharp
I know this
and I won't do it again
or so
I tell myself
but it's comfortable
having the option
having the back door
the Plan K.

no one is coming for me
no one will call
all I have is myself
and for right now

that is not enough;
for now
I am not strong.

the blade kisses my wrist
my toes, my ankles
like the Her before last
and all I want
is to call it;
a giant beanstalk
ladder
up or down.

call me
another
doctor.
the others won't return
my messages.
Maybe I hide it too well
they think that I am fine,
though they might
have an inkling.
they probably have
some kind of clue.

they don't see
the crimson streams,
the bare, purple knuckles.

while I know
that my persistence
will win the life,
today no one loves
any kind of me
and tomorrow will
be much the same.
I haven't left this studio
for days.

This blade looks sharp
like coals begging
to burn soft, pink
soles of organs.
This blade looks like the only
healthy relationship
I've had in a while.

And that's slicing something.

damn shame

I want to cry
I do
they just don't come
like aborted pregnancies
coagulating at the base
of oil slick condoms,
the moisture hangs in reserve
pragmatic
handling the poison adamantly
pushing through my veins
rather than
handling the venom
seeping from your words
and torrentially flowing
through my memories.

Catharsis never felt so much
like cancer.

I'd love the release of crying
as much as I hate the wasted
borrowed time
you left me with; that you left
with him
with.

I'd love to cry.
But it seems the only organs
in my body that know better
enough not to
are my tear ducts
and the eyes that see
truths out of sweet nothings.

Yes, I'd love to hate you,
and I'd love to cry
but
the borrowed time has been billed
and I'm left paying
the check
with a declined credit card
checks of self-pity
and loose change
as if the tears were somehow
not worth paying for
anymore.

ritualistic shame mongering

I watched her face burn
from the center

of a dusty gravel parking lot
the sad smile stemming
from my presence in her life
contorting into gruesome
plastic bubbles
and lighting up my face
the way she used to
before the empty parking
lot in my chest
was littered with trash
and ashes.

I watched unflinching
as the face of the woman
crumbled to dust
reminiscent of the last kiss
I ever received
from such a beautiful mistake.

As I sit here lamenting
all of the lessons learned
I can't help but think
of this happenstance
as a microcosm of the way
everything ends:
down, in flames.

As these words roll onto the
faded, dented, crumpled
yellow pages
the knock on the door
jars an uneasy mind.
I know it is the new thing
but I wish
time and time again
that it was her.
that the whole nightmare
that surgically yet savagely

sliced out the best chunk
of heart that I could have offered
would be over,
and that I could raise my head
out of the thorny mess
of hands, nails and brambles
my eyes opening onto an
impossibly angelic face
I thought I knew
for such a long, long time.

I let the new Her walk down the stairs
just as She let me fall down
The Hill, tumbling into
the Canyon of Hell
laughing as the man
she betrayed
detonated on impact;
laughing in ecstatic glee
as the remnants
of bones and flesh
rained around her,
sinking down
to the parched red ground
in flames.

I don't blame her.

All I can see now
are the pieces of the photograph
jettisoned from the whole
by the taciturn breeze
doing it's best to put out
the smoldering ashes
clinging to the legs of a man
hell-bent
on igniting;
hell-bent on watching

the whole damn thing
burn.

<u>on the rails</u>

The train is a floating home
bouncing along the rail
jovially, without a care
for the rest of the hurried,
harried and harrowed world.
The trains just keep running
as if walking, pacing
as if strutting, catching
the breeze as if drifting,
wings angled sharply
towards the sky.

This train is a migrating bird,
aloft on a warm bed
of thermals and uplifts,
journeying toward some kind
of hallowed ground trodden
on countless times
by ancestors it will never know,
for reasons it is oblivious to,
much like the bright-faced travelers
in it's gullet.

If it knew where it was
headed to, would the train
still resolutely fly
in that particular direction?
Or would it veer off
on a course of it's own?
Would it feel shackled
to the ancient routine?
Or would it proudly follow
the well-trodden paths

of it's ancestors?
Would it try to shake off
the parasitic passengers
from it's steel-clad spine
like a frantically bucking
caterpillar?
Would it expel its' guts
like a frog spewing a tainted
stomach from its mouth
like bubble gum?
Or would it happily engage
it's fate, as a loyal horse?
If it had it's own mind
would the train become more
than the rails?

Would it become more than
those floating faces
bellowing
"Home, Sweet Home!"
echoing the sentiments
of barnacles encrusting
the sides of such a humpback?

Would it get to know
such parasitic fixtures,
the cream of the crap,
as I
want
to know?

Would it question
it's own fate
as I do?

Would it be
a dynamite
conversationalist?

Perhaps such a fate
is much like our own,
sentenced to wander aimlessly
toward a vaguely defined goal,
a hazily remembered nesting ground;
the Babylon Hotel.

All I know
is that until I find such a place
or until this train begins to speak
actual words
this is the closest I will get
to 'home'.
As I float
toward the nowhere of middling
I will continue to ply the minds
of my fellow barnacles
for the next great idea,
passing out beer
like water to refugees
and sleeping on the floor
between the benches,
ultimately finding
that while the destination is
indeed the short-term
goal,
it is the journey that teaches you
the importance of being.

I have a feeling
my bucking caterpillar friend
would agree.

All aboard.

And they tell me I'm wicked
anger seeps from my bones.
A man with the means
to only sound vicious,
till he bleeds tears
and he has no more wishes,
till the well runs dry
and he's cobbled by stone.

rip tide

In the rain the persevering fire just won't die. Go figure.
Before the clouds loomed, dry drift wood was piled in stacks
as if the previous night's high tide had made an honest
attempt at generosity. In my overwhelming genius I had
decided to collect as much of these gifts as I could in order to
play Prometheus. As the drizzle began to make it through the
dense pines under which I had situated my meager camp I
had the bright idea to leap for the sun, before my pile became
too damp. Now unstoppably ablaze, smoke pouring from the
tiered center in a constant plume, the menace remains
staunchly emboldened. After repeated threats of the
permanent loss of my sight and enough tears to drown the
rest of the dry needles underneath my boots, I decided to take
a walk. As any semi-responsible, pseudo-boyscout would do.

Immediately after turning the corner I was whipped across
the face by a slashing wind, carrying the hearty drops across
the sandy expanse in obvious defiance to my previous godly

endeavors. It was in the midst of this environmental berating that I noticed the drag marks, as if I had just missed some very important business. Business that involves someone who at one point was burdened with too much money who is now burdened with two cement blocks. And a rising tide.

Instead of any mob related festivities, however, even as I began to think of my own mild distaste of swimming in chains, I was met with a sight far less adventuresome. Staring at me were two impossibly sad eyes, two furtively struggling fin-arms and one thoroughly miserable body, shaking in what was obviously the final pangs of life.

A sea otter had come ashore to die.

As I stared, it stared back. Our eyes locked in a tug-of-war between man and beast, heart and heart. As the latter faltered I became stronger. The circle of life, I guess. I wondered if, when this seal was just a pup, it's father had taken it to the highest rock that they could shimmy up to and said:

"Someday, my son, this will all be yours."

I wonder if it had had a seahorse and a thickheaded tuna as two lighthearted yet cowardly companions.

Those eyes though. They still burn through my memory as a soldier's last wish gone unfulfilled. They still plead with me to do it. "Just **do it**!" They screamed. "Please." And for a while, standing in the sideways rain and pacing next to that goddamn smokeferno I called a campfire, I considered it.

Was it the possibility of being wrong that stayed my hand? Was it the laws that govern the treatment of endangered species? Was it cowardice? Or was it my own hakuna-ma-fucking-tata?

When I returned to the surf line I saw that the poor bastard had dragged itself even further up onto the sand. Crows stood not twenty feet away, perched in the first stand of trees on the edge of the beach. An eagle circled above, clearly weighing its options. As I watched the scene play out the otter raised its head, still shaking. That same stare. Those same damn eyes. I turned, incapable. Looking over my shoulder I saw that it was still pleading, desolation drooling from its mouth. Maybe it was just the tremors rocking it's rapidly deteriorating frame, but I swear the otter shook its head from side to side, as if saying:

"No. Don't go."

Just do it. I couldn't. My hands began to shake. The wind and rain, already drenching the rain inundated scene, picked up. I turned my head and quick-stepped back to my camp. As I looked back I saw the crows begin to edge closer. The eagle began to circle lower. My eyes, already strained, began to water.

And the fire, albeit temporarily, went out.

<u>19</u>

This is my youth
myself
the transference
and transvergence
of a wandering, transient
mind
caterwauling
between several notions of success

and a finicky personage
that personifies
the very notion
of capitalization.

Here I sit.
The ideals of goals and illusory
successes
transcendent
in only the sense
of the words themselves,
fixated
on one thing,
and one thing only,
pussy.
As it has always been.

This is why I am
no ladies
man.

I love. I traverse. '
I walk. I talk.
I give out my number.
As if they'll call me back.
As if, even if,
we got along,
they would consider
staying
for long
even though the notion of permanence
hadn't been completely eradicated
from a mind barren
of all such hopeful
and irrational
contrivances.

Call me a misanthrope.

Call me a shrink that will
answer my calls.

I am young and I certainly
do my best
to continue living
yet the point
remains illusory.

As if the nonexistent
is omnipresent
and the all-seeing deity
is toying with me.

Fuck 'em.

I'll go down with the ship.

But I will go down,
in the charade of youth
yelling and haranguing
as if someone gives
a damn.

As if there's a point
to this whole
growing old
shit.

letting loose

A friend tells me to tear out,

just let it rip, to step outside
and just scream, roar, shred the air
as loud as I can
with no heed for any kind of reaction
or resonance
that I might create.

He tells me he did this the other night.
He lives next door to me.
This was definitely the reason
I jumped out of bed
thinking that the age old nightmare
of those people that I can still love
all dying in their very own
pools of blood
had finally materialized.

He tells me to just go; just do it.
Get out there and scream bloody
murder from the top of my lungs
to the bottom,
to let my soul just bare all
with a bare chest crossed
only by the arms of grace and
sweet, sweet justice
as if such an intangible element
could be shot out of a cannon
at all those slackjawed little pissant,
teetotalling, miserably wayward
gravel-brained and piss-stained mattresses
could comprehend
such a message
anyway.

What my friend doesn't know
is that I am so close to the edge,
so close to tearing
all the damn time

that it is a constant battle
to remain on a even keel
to not fight every single person
I see
to death
in the street
with a HUGE FUCKING SMILE
ON MY GODDAMN FACE
BLOOD DRIPPING BETWEEN
MY GODDAMN TEETH

DO YOU FUCKING UNDERSTAND ME.

What my friend does not understand
is that if I stepped out on that balcony,
bare chested and barreling,
and began to scream from the bottom
of my lungs and soul to the very top
I would never, ever be able
to stop
and that
that
particular train
would keep rolling
until the whole damn, soul-fulfilling
ride
would be a bloodbath of epic proportions.

So for now,
my friend
I think I'll stay mum.

Yeah.

caught staring

Was that you looking over this way
across the inches of dried beer
sticking unmercifully to the bar
just glancing casually
without any expression
as I smiled in your direction?

Was that you moving to the corner
away from the casual Jezebel
and the two meat bags pretending
to be funny as they pretended
to laugh and listen?

Was that you who stared at me
through my shades and yours
as I told you about my home,
about how you would
be perfect in my life
er
city?

Was that you who grabbed my hands
and clasped them
tightly, as if hanging
from a helicopter above concrete?
Who took my face in both hands
after texting your boyfriend
my phone number
and kissed me like I was your
first glass of water?

Was that you who walked off,
away from that beach, bar, bustle

away from the jackass tourists and
hustling locals, swinging your hips
side to side
like an excited pendulum
briefly silhouetted in the sun?

Was it me who stayed?

one and the same

there's a man
outside the window
smoking a rolled cigarette
as awkwardly
as I would.

it certainly is
strange
how he stands there,
crocodile Dundee hat
and everything,
frantically
huffing and puffing
on a drooping
coffin
while tossing a
bouncy ball
against the window,
ostensibly to get
the pretty girl's
(sitting next to me)
attention.

he stops,
turns,
and exhales through his
nose, the curls
of smoking frothing
from his bushy beard
like spilled mead.

the thought
permeating my mind
is the pervading desire to
grow a mane
of my own.

soon, he sits on a chair
right outside the window,
still
bouncing that silly
little ball
affecting nothing
but his own misappropriated
sense of chivalry.

maybe I have too much hair
already.

when the girl
fails to notice his
patient antics
he changes tactics and
pretends to ride
a hog of epic
proportions.

oh, if only I had thought of that.

in between changing gears and

looking into his rearviews,
the girl is gone but,
still
I cant help but
cheer and
laugh along.

we do,
after all,
ride the same motorcycle.

Missy Missy Mays

Her name flowed nicely off the tongue
just as I would imagine how her skin
would roll nicely off of mine.
Like a folk singer
or the friendly and homily beautiful
girl behind the counter at some
assbackwards truckstop
in the middle of the desert.

It was New Orleans, so when I asked
whether she knew where The Tree was
she smiled, dropped her heavy briefcase off
and walked me and my light guitar
straight there.
The gnarled roots gave me a seat as her dogs
rolled lazily at my feet,
she standing below me a little nervously
as if the heat clung to her hands
the same way they made her shirt

cling to her damp skin.

As she smiled at me I felt the sunshine
crashing through the overhanging limbs,
thick rays of lolling enthusiasm
splayed over an otherwise hopelessly lethargic
atmosphere.
It seemed like such a sure thing.
I could see her considering the possibilities.
How her animals had been the only ones
companioning her
for such a long time. How she just wanted
wanted, wanted
and how I was right in front of her
singing all kinds of love songs
that she could just fall right into
head first.

She texted me all day,
even stopping by my perch later on to
drop a coke in my hand
before the indecision kicked right back in
and she was off again,
on some kind of errand she couldn't define
even to her dogs in the back seat
as mine clutched the back of the case
just waiting to be walked
and taken
all kinds of care of.

I mean, come on.
It was New Orleans.
In spring time.
We were adults.
In our prime.
There was pollen
lightly drifting along
on the magical carpet

of a southern afternoon breeze.

We went out for a drink, after
the inevitable awkward meeting
with her neighbors, the woman
just looking off to the side
her meaning
clear as a glacial lake
that I would soon be swimming in.

The drinks were weak
the bar pretentious
and the atmosphere strained
until we were walking and the
goddamn indecision flaring
between us as we walked
as if hand in hand
straight to her door,
when I had to leave.

I waited, telling her that I would
come right back
if she wanted.
That my back rubs
were legendary.

"Ready."
She replied.
I was there in fifteen minutes.
When I called her to let me in
she was confused.
Baffled and bemused.
I reiterated the supposed phone conversation.
She rushed over as I waited down the block.
And believe me, believe me, please
just believe me
I'd have been ashamed if I was still capable.
When I saw her I explained. She just

smiled, smiled, smiled.
She told me
that well, well, well
you'll be here for four more days,
right?

I'm leaving in the morning.
I replied.

"Well, you're so..."
And I was walking to the car.
"...back and...."
And the car started up.
I loved that car.
"...forth..."
And the car was in drive.
"...with that..."
Goodbye, darlin'.

So much for some Big Easy.

I checked the calendar.
It was May.
May?
I'd been there for months.

I liked this one though.

I raced home, head down,
chin up
slept the sleep of the
innocent damned
and left before the sunrise.

swiping

I saw your picture today
trying to smile at
as they crowded around
your goggles, mask and
bloodshot eyes
like vultures
and I admired it.
I hold no such pretenses
snatching a grimace
just hoping to snap
for one person to
say something
out of line
so that I can create
more hairline fractures
along popped knuckles
and a tin can hull
carrying me away.

Every flight today has
come complete with a pretty
girl alongside
the universe taunting me
as if saying
here's what you could
have had
here's what she could
have looked like
sleeping alongside your
spread legs
rather than masked and hooded
surrounded
and the rocking

air conditioner
whispers in tune
to the passing horizon:
she could have been
here
she could have been
here
with you
she could have been
real
Sam.

Sam?

second languages

Her eyes tell the story,
but whether or not I am the protagonist
is anyone's guess.
She had never kissed a man before,
a fact I could tell
by the way her face contorted
into a suckerfish
any time I
leaned in.

Behold, the struggle.

At any point in life a man
begins to be bombarded
with requests and the tacit beckonings
of soft hands and cherubic faces.

While the world is a cruel place
there are still those that are born
to rise as stalwarts; as illuminating beacons
for how it should be.

Given that a Good Man is cast
in such a mold,
one would be prone to imagine
that all such men are weak
and innocent.
What is neglected in such thinking
is that opening one's self
to perceived weakness,
letting the cruelties of life smack you
right in the face,
heart and soul,
over and over and over again,
makes a man tougher
than you can possibly imagine.

I can survive anywhere.
I can force the world
to be a better place.
And I can teach this girl
how to kiss me.
And then some.

When she sees me, I know.
I feel the childish yearnings tempered
by equally childish social constraints.
My balls feel the pull; my mind the need
And still, I am reduced
to a boot camp
kissing instructor.

She tells me that she is 21.
I check her passport.

As she beckons me into her room
I become aware
of the Hello Kitty sheet covers
the multi-colored sock arrangements
and the Victoria Secret hand bags
carefully stowed underneath
the sagging bunks; the pink laces
carefully sprawled out toward
the dull yellow lights overhanging
this torpedo tube.

She laughs nervously
and wags her head from side to side.
I can feel the microbeads of sweat
seeping from her pores.
As she swings back and forth, it's hard
not to be weary, but a good teacher
never gets frustrated
and never gives in to the tedium.

Her eyes may tell the story,
but I am the one who writes it.

threads through empty veins

I remember climbing up the pinnacle
one hand on the steep shale
one hand an inch away from
your impossibly perfect ass
and the sun
wanly smiling on both
of our smiling faces.

I still thought that you were fucking
that other guy
and you still thought that
I was *such* a moron for it
and nothing too bad
had happened just yet.

She had come back.
Ostensibly to see me.
It was doomed and we both knew it
but for the first time
I couldn't think of anything
but the sweet nectar of time and breath
widening my arteries
and the certainty
that whenever the hell I felt like it
I could tap into the purest drinking water
the world has ever known.
I could drown in it
once per last breath
and I did
for all I cared.

I remember how my entire life
once so carefully planned and mapped
became a loose assortment of tentative goals
each more far-reaching than the last
a collection of constantly collapsing tiers
just begging to be stacked
one atop the other
on my way up the mountain of her mind.
All that I wanted fit between my arms.
I did not care whether there were any chips on the table,
not to mention whether or not
they lay down
in a way particular to me
in particular.

We fucked on top of that pinnacle
just to say that I
that we
had literally and figuratively
been there and done that.
There.
I remember thinking that I was simultaneously
the luckiest and unluckiest man in the world.
Just the concept made my face numb.

I've been alone since
then and
yes, it lasted a while after
that
and then it ended in
screams and supernova
and then it lingered
and then the others weren't good enough
and then there was no one
to be had
at all
and then
isolation
as far away as I could get
and then I wrote this
sitting alone in a room
at the very top
the pinnacle
one hand on the edge of the bed
the other on the keys
my back to the paper thin walls and
my mind left to wander off the edge
of such a perfectly formed tower
of pictures and
elevated stories.

goals

every day is less clear
another jumbled, hodgepodge goal
thrown at the wall
in the hopes that one day
a break in the clouds
would allow enough sunshine in
to make it stick.
on the island it all made sense
the sweltering heat bringing toxic
thoughts and sludge through
every damned pore
as a form of salvation.
there it was easy and now
$9.87
and change
to my name
the beauty of starting from 0
is rattling my stomach, my nerves
and my will
and while the goal no longer hovers
illusory in context
the sky remains clear of rain-stuffed pillows
ready to spurt whiskey
and the hours pass as baby steps
toward a future
far more imaginable.

<u>cold and cloudy, I think</u>

It always just felt good
comforting
a blanket less restrictive
just to have it on and feel the air
coursing across a rug of skin and hair
swaying as if contented.
In this hotel, back and forth,
just like every other hotel
in the
middle
of somewhere
I never really could remember,
and here we are,
so far away from one another
and any dreams or
middle
ground we could have shared
just left to drift on that wind
that courses
sometimes
through the heater underneath
my legs
just like the words
cast disrespectively on the white
simulated page
staring me in the face
as if trying to
start
a fight.

Good
thing
I know better

than to fight
my own fingers
or the sky
even if there is
a temperature
button
chokehold
conveniently misplaced
or a whole day's worth
of cheap beer and
unnecessary things
to worry about
in
this place so far
away from home and
so close
to a heater I think
i'm going to have to leave on
just about
all day.

at a time

I spent my last nine dollars on beer
the ice still clinging to the bottle
as I walked onto the wrong bus
and the memory of coins
clinking in my backpack
four miles
and an hour and a half away
jingling through my pockets
as if they were full.

I am 26 years old.
I sold everything I own.
I am penniless.

For some reason I am still smiling
half way through the six pack
alone in a basement room
I pay pennies on the dollar for
despite the cracked window
and the room adjacent full of
laughing girls
who have yet to join me in
abject solitude.

Because once upon a time I had a dream
to go out and see the world
and it seemed as if everything that could
hold me by the back of my belt
did so, and with gusto
talons gripped into my spine
as if trying to force feed
yet when the chips were down
the rain poured
hookers walking me up the street
and the locals looking at my soaked shirt
with pity and attempted understanding
then it clicked.

Adventure is for those with something to lose.
Those of us who just like to wander
however
so do in those places in which
wandering is an application of one's soul
of one's wanderlust
of the appreciation that the world is a beautiful
woman worth exploring
with or without shoes

but definitely with
beer in one hand,
balls in the other.

<u>really should</u>

you should have
seen your face

you should have
seen mine

the grand opera that conducted itself
through flailing, slashing arms
was ours
for a minute
all vibrations of matter and course
combusting quickly into
an insidious contempt
snarled petulantly across
two bloody, barren bodies.

I should have kept my mouth shut.

it's a relative truth
that love and hate
are so intimately intertwined.

when all is said and done the
door shatters and the sun rises
announcing the first day without
you and your ski ramp nose
and homemade cookies
and those pink panties with the flower on the top
that I could take off with my teeth.

i play doctor
a solipsism enema scathing my insides
coating my gut with steel, complete

with a titanium hernia
chuckling like a deranged clown
holding a smoking gun.

without bullets, guns are just distractions
and we all know
mouths shoot blanks.

I know you miss me
and I share the sentiment.
I miss me too.

I go to bed with
someone else who bores me.
She doesn't snore, kick or
itch my face with her hair
but somehow I sleep less than ever,
as if some kind of nuisance is necessary
to keep from paying attention
to a sickeningly sweet nostalgia
who would have thought that
such an asshole had such a monstrous
soft-spot for succubi.

if only you could
see my face.

if only I could
see yours.

counter terrorism

in a class
of roughly
400
I watched a video
of soldiers hovering
above some barren
Iraqi village.

the soldiers' monotonous
voices
coming through over the
PA system of the auditorium
sounded much
like
what I would imagine
packs of dogs
sound to each other
on the hunt.

the video
depicting a long range
strike on
suspected
terrorism
as the bombs exploded,
the crosshairs fixed on locations
directly in front
of the fleeing,
terrified,

suspects,

the instructor hid his

boner
and
the operators laughed,
and laughed and
laughed
and the class
of 400
laughed with them.

one particular image showed,
in the white glare of the
infrared targeting device
a missile detonating within
two feet
of a running white
blob.

the blob,
needless to say,
detonated in an
equally violent and
catastrophic manner,
its' limbs
flying in all directions.

someone clapped
and cheered,
as if their
team
had won the Superbowl.

someone tell the
family of this
blob
that its'
killers
did not even know
its' face

when they erupted
its'
organs out through
its'
trachea and

laughed.

got em, the operator said,
laughing,
laughing
laughing.

these
operators,
hovering over a land
I probably couldn't locate
on a nameless map
fight like
gods
for a purpose
ill defined,
at best
for a nation
watching events unfold
in much the same
manner.
a nation supposedly built
on Christian taboos
of false gods
and idolatry,
fashions itself as
Gods.

and we all know,
Gods are the ones who
write history and
dictate justice.

I guess that
is
pretty funny.

why a waste of words

why
does the landslide always
promote another
more brutal
form of erosion.

walking through the
motions
paces
and solemn echoes of
footsteps
quickly disappearing
I find
no solace in the
grim satisfaction
of an
impending release.

it is
rather becoming
of such a desolate
undertaking
such as life
that one's
fortitude is challenged

by one's own
fortifications.

how
(on earth)
could something so
twisted and diabolic
such as

solitude

have such a
recurrent transfer rate?

it must be some kind of magic
that draws the
hope from your
twisted innards and
wrings it out
into the malignant
disease that
drinks you.

as hilarious as it
seems
I believe
(if I have
ever believed)
that it is the
dignity in trenchancy
that fuels such
a lackadaisical meteor
to rise again,
if only to slide
back
back
back
down

the page.

fare and blight

the streets whip past
in a blur
just a kaleidoscope
of grime, half working
traffic lights
and the immutable
presence of nothing for nothing
the taxi drivers
smile and drop me off
this is my fifth ride tonight
there will be nine
saying "coca, aqui."
and I have no idea
what the hell I am doing
out this particular juncture
I have no clue
as to where my money
is quickly draining
but the chalky drip
coats my throat as sewage
and the need
presses
my frontal lobes, chaining
my hippocampus to the promise
of more German pussy
and the cab driver seeks
furtively
just another failed mission
from the get-go
but I'm leaning
toward the middle
the seat caving
much like a rock slide

till he's letting me out
not laughing
and I hold a smirk
like two coins
ready to roll into palms
greased
but ready
to stop sliding.

this whole time
I thought I was
facing rejection
when
the face of reflection
showed I was
only
lacking my own
acception.

(whistling)

this whole time
I cringed when
they laughed.
I couldn't
take
the fact that the
world
wants nothing to
do with my
nonsense
unless I make
it worth their while.

and I don't plan on
doing anything
like that.

what a thought.

talking you down

too many people have counted on me
for such a wide array of
trivialities and needs
not realizing
it's impossible to tell someone
reaching out for you to save them
at least for a moment
that you, blessed with the sacred remedies,
that there are no answers
and rather that
success, love and sunshine
are all products of an illegible universe
acting in ways dictated by
an immeasurable chaos.

it's impossible to tell
someone that
nothing is impossible
but rather that
any action, reaction
or transient property is
the sole
responsibility of
inertia.

it's impossible to tell
someone something,
with any sort of validity,
a concept or notion that
one cannot apply to
one's own mind.

how trite it seems

that of
all the people
who have needed me
the one who
needed
me most
was myself.

and i'm supposed to
help.
myself.
right?

It has occurred to me
often and rapidly
that I should
cast off my phone
much like
shedding a layer of skin.
the tears that
have been squeezed like
acid from a lemon rind,
in the same manner
as a spider with a
fresh meal,
have fallen without
my hand to brush them
off of cheeks and
delicate necks.
the phone represents
a medium through
which to
weigh down my
heavy mind with
the troubles of
a catastrophically flawed
societal menagerie.

I mean
with the iExtension of
arms and thumbs
we believe we have become
transcendent of nature
we have become
all that we
could ever hope to dream
on the shitter
or
wiping scraped knees
or
crying in person to
3D friends.

we are
after all
just animals.
and somehow,
I have become more
animal
than the rest.
if such a thing is
humanly possible.

alive again

frozen atop the crumbling rock
two squirrels eye their death
a red-tailed specter, a bird of prey
alert straddling the breath
of a breeze illuminated

by the shining rays of day
and it sure ain't surprising
but it surely is a shame
that the caterwauling black machine
that tows this grand 'ol scythe
that whereupon the order deemed
on the talons of this life
soft as a million blades of grass
as double sided as the knife
and here we find us standing
beckoning a breeze
to carry us from shadows
to rise us off our knees
so here's to such petulance
among the jaws of the end
it is here that we learn to dance
it is here we make our friends
for such staunch refusals
of the inherent reprisals of fear
can only help us live these lives
and get these bushy tails in gear.

graduating

the bus rumbles,
soothing aching muscles
and minds
escaping the mindless
death of a small
town convinced it
was meant for something
bigger,

better,
farther.

I sway, back and
forth to the rhythm
of a transit
designed to save the
highways from
overuse and
the inevitable repairs
always somehow made
ever more
necessary.

it's a sunny fucking day
and I will
learn today
to leave you, your
maladaptive ambitions and
the concerted efforts of
150,000
to keep me down,

behind.

these roads serve
as the costly
reminder of
just what it takes
exactly
to operate a trans-city
social monopoly
that I
have no subscription to.

if only we could all
let it all hang out.

if only there was some
neon sign
highlighting the
long road
to peace and serenity.

what a shame.
what a pity.
what a goddamn miracle.

there are
bigger,
better
and farther
and I plan to use
the rest of my life
to find
some of them.
as I sit on
this bus
I cant help but
force the
spent memories
out the window and
onto the narrow strip of
concrete designed
for emergencies.

I hope they planned for
the screaming, crying
jeering, mundane and
asinine characteristics of
a 150,000 strong
accident.

I'm glad I was
never very good at math.

to me,
all that matters is
that gray line
leading me up and away
from such a barren
stretch of highway
as that.

godsend

i'd like to believe that
I
am some kind of
esoteric godsend.

i'll bet you'd
like
to believe that too.

if I was
I could give you
some kind
of insight that you
you
could apply to your own
life for the next fifteen
minutes and then
forget till
you
read it again.

it's a shame,

that wishes can't be
eaten
so I continue
walking and writing
walking and writing
walking and dying
again
on a barren screen
devoid of
warmth and affection
for the amusement of
the crowds I
entertain inside
my eyes

you're just part
of the show.

the crowd sighs,
and I snap the spine
of this tentative idea

the one where any of this has meaning.

this chair- bolts, wood and
all the intangibles,
will stand till it
erodes from the
neverending queue of
ass fat and hair,
the ancient trees outside
will wave until they are
inevitably slain
by the fumes and clouds of smoke
billowing from the
river of steel pouring
through the
channel underneath and

this place will
someday fall,
crashing benignly into a
pool of books, marble and
tired souls still
dying to stay.

the rain roars, the city whispers and
the train hits another
mangy dog in an exposition of
movement amongst blithe chaos.

it's a good day to be a
cynic.

but you knew all this.

now
don't you
wish
I was an esoteric godsend
or do you
like me
wonder just what
the point
of not having a
point
really is
anymore.

the x in expresso

I walk into a
cliche French
crepe and coffee shop
the only one on the block
that has seats
outside
so I don't have to look
listen or touch
any of the people who
also
take advantage of
good coffee and
free internet.

immediately i'm
awkward
as a girl from high school,
one of those people you
tried
to be cordial to,
avoids my gaze as if
I ever wanted to see her
disfigured personality
ever again.

i would have burned them all
within that school
if given the
opportunity.

who me?

I make the mistake of

fidgeting and biting a
fat bottom lip.
these types of moments
make me question
yet again
whether or not
I was ever human.
I grab my coffee and
head outside
where,
naturally,
there she stands,
awkwardly avoiding my gaze.

I've been trying to be social
lately, i.e.
ive been acting like
a fool
lately so I
make the mistake
of saying her name.

Immediately,
I sighed.

She noticed.

Maybe its time to make some coffee at home.

Or just find a new
place to plug in.

set a minute

Bus to bus to train to cab
to rooftop hostel
with a very, very
tall beer
and a view over Quito
rolling hills languidly sluiced
down to the city center
perched atop of which
is one weary gringo
just waiting now
for the first tenets
of an elusive normalcy
if one can define
anything in these parts
as such
let this beer dwindle
get another
get this man a cigarette
and he will be Hunter
minus the Panama
and the veritable
high tide of humanity
can cross below
as buses
trains
motos
and taxis
as this very, very tall beer
disappears
and, finally,
I'm here.

<u>back</u>

it is
such a shame
that such ferocity
could be wasted
on such a lackadaisical
creature such as
i

i
have seen so many

actions, reactions and
syllables blindly uttered
i
could fill a sewage truck
with bile-stained nails.

i could.

it's like having a
pan in your chest that
is
constantly boiling over and
rising upwards
through the tangles of organs
to your temples,

where it waits

it's only the beloved that
are eventually beheaded
by a dull guillotine.

what we would do.

some say that hate and love
are the same

all I know is
that they can be used
regularly and with
uncanny effectiveness
against unsuspecting
assholes.

it's like watching a pan
in someone's chest
that is constantly boiling over
and rising
upwards,
boiling their eyes and
leaving throbbing
red boils on the outsides
of their shredded fingernails.

it's like watching a gnat
flounder in a birdbath.

but she can
yell louder than
you

but
even if it made
some kind
of difference, she wouldn't
do it
anyway.

isn't that
just it?

extroverted introvert

I watch these people
I meet these people
you couldn't dream of
it's just me
and
the shine
I meet everyone
at least once
judgment flies
out the window like
disposable food
as if
such a meal
was dispensable
I meet such people
who go out
into the world
and make as they want it
money become paramount to
girls
and
making it happen
becomes the real currency
they always invite me down
to their home
to see what it's like
and I try to
explain
that its not the same here
really i've just grown used to
the incapabilities
that drive me
an hour ago I had to

tell a girl
I didn't have time
an event I would never
dream about
one year ago
yet the power that lies
in the decision to
remain aloof and
unattached
empowers you, until
you're alone in your room
chicken pecking at some
keyboard
talking to a bright screen
and feeling according to
the music put on
as I've done since
I can remember
maybe the difference between
me and the people I
so envy
is a willingness
to leave emotion, the driving
force behind such feelings of
want and need
behind as you progress towards becoming a
better human being.
while we have
readily discovered that
no such purpose exists
there is no greater love than the
love generated from exceeding
in one's path
be that the path
as it may
discarded along that path, it
still remains
as an

however illusory
trench towards salvation
I don't know
the most common phrase
ever uttered
becomes the dogma
ever a stalwart
as I contemplate
exactly
how I sidestepped
as the kids with girls
go home to warm beds and warm thighs.

all I ever was
was myself.

as such, I sit alone and
type
type
type
a child left with only
words to utter
on a barren page
disheartened to the point where
I don't know what
course of action to take
yet the best option seems to
be
losing myself in the
imparted chemicals of my mind
drawing myself into a
virtual coma, in
which I move amongst a
gooey mob that repulses against
when I do something
strange
giving the mover no momentum and
leaving

only the most brash
to pick up the pieces and the
rest of us
drunk and philosophic
in our bedrooms.

can't go home now

it's hit me today
several times like file cabinets
slamming open to a wild protrusion
of waxed brown file folders and the
rainbow array of tags marking section
and importance
i'm not an innocent
if anyone ever was
i'm not a victim
like the pasty white, terror stricken
Dracula victims, too doused in lace and
pearls to raise the helpless hand
anyway
i've pointedly and decidedly drawn my
rudder on deck and
i've derisively shadowed the
would be sirens of the
precious
sunlight,
engulfing the shallow dignity of
the chain-held light bulb, swinging
to the insistently tugging swells
with a pale patience blatantly
glimmering with unutterable

utterances.

the ocean runs deep in my blood like
iron fused to the edge of
a plasma life raft.
i'm hopelessly intertwined with
the Caribbean
addiction
the cardboard keeled gamble
and a bottomless, insatiable
thirst for direction.
love is the curves in the blanket
against the perfectly etched horizon
reaching on through to the
lines of my cinnamon hair, course
with salt and long with cold
aging never felt this
good
i know the pill kills me
but it works for killing aches and pains.
i figure i'm just pushing my luck,
and sailing.

fastidious, delirious and
defiant
denuded then sheared
peeled as so many pounds
of spuds are peeled
my opened pores expunge
indignation, my veins
pulse with a virulent protest
until my heart aches and
detonates.
I am a cheap roman candle.
first potential, now
I am kinetic, actively
glued to the sheets in order
to calm the fuck down.

Hannah

she explodes in my head as
everything I need
right now
our eyes are boring into
the depth of haziness
we stare blindly
as my fondness takes a leap
of faith in the passenger
seat of my car
my hair holds the faint
scent of cigarettes
that she loves
my fingers of the inside
of my presumptuous
infatuation
and my hands of the warmth
seizing the holes
perforating the symmetry
of my eagerly anticipating
frame
I can't help but let myself
feel comfortable and
at ease
as if something marvelous
has occurred while
I've sat square in the center
of her
directed eyes
solid and visible.

gravel

this tiny little island,
not nearly a mile across
this is where I made my stand
this is where I could run no further,
no longer,
in fact
I couldn't when I tried.
This lonely paradise,
Pergatory's Waiting Room
a retirement community of croquet and carrion
in the dirty, unkempt white sand
dotted with hungry sea birds
is where I said

no, dammit
I will not run!
I will NOT be pushed around.
I will not lose!
NO GODDAMN YOU FUCKING FUCK YOUS
I WILL NOT LOSE!!!!
screamed like a tantrum but rather
more like a strike of lightning
flashing between illusory prisms
from the built up bullshit
straining at the seams
to fertilize.

no longer will these failures, falls,
capitulations
continue to hang across my shoulders
like a burden of shame, like that goddamn rain
I will never go back to.

I know that now.

They tried to fire me, before I quit
a conclusion everyone could see
before anyone had ever
even set eyes on one another
General Grant's first offensive
on a tired and misanthropic
talent pool
and yet this boat, jumpy
on the choppy swells
does not argue
and as the seas have always known
sometimes the best option
is to rise up
devastate
and recede
always present yet sometimes
tumultuous in the nature
of swelling to something
as staunchly unimpeded
as the weather
as Hurricane Sam
as life
and as one roustabout
makes a stand
as he walks away.

Rachel

They were just castles of sand and cards
evidently

they were just guns left to rust
these golden roads to the slaughter factory
where we could remove enough organs
to stay together
had tolls and busted tires
and you cant fight
you have to get up in the morning and smile
all day you cant say a word
you cant cook with butter
there arent enough chaffers to polish
to make this buffet feast happen
so here it goes down the canyon
jump the moon and blue paint
spread it in finger prints
across others cheeks paint your face
so they won't notice, they won't hear
so you can scream some more.

Suddenly the bubble pops
we're sleeping on the floor on mats and blankets
you tried so hard to try so hard
and my arm is around you, my side slipping to the floor
just a fading memory
at this point
the tickets are bought, your mind is made
the canyon echoes and beckons, a six pack away
from new people entirely
the snow starts to fall and skates cut through
a melting haze, humid in a dry heat
sandwiches and stolen beers replace
a laugh gone presence gone kisses before work gone
contented
nights
gone
and the house is packed, vacuumed with precision
my stuff cast across houses and garages
and you're right in front of me
a walking house of sand and cards

kisses gone hugs gone lies gone silence
and I'm gone.

How 'Bout That

I'm only laughing because you
didn't understand what I said.
You didn't get it.
I need to get home
take a shower
the warm water should
unhinge my shoulders;
leave me spotless
and untainted.

I do not know what I am
going to do about this
sometimes even I can't understand
the mumbles coming from
the ground
and sometimes
interruptions
let me futilely stare at the wall
in frustration while I listen
to the blathering chorus line
of
life is a bitch and then you die.

"How 'bout that."
I say to them, because
of the store clerk I once knew
who said that after
every transaction.
He was selling
amenities to suits who
didn't get it,
while he laughed because
he didn't get it

either.
He wrote biographies
in his spare time
I'm glad
neither of us
quit our day job.
Now I sit here
'home' in the shower,
the irony laughing to my face
and whispering
always whispering
How 'bout that Sam,

how fuckin' 'bout that.

<u>hot streak</u>

Naked, I am the bottom
rung of my subsistence,
satisfied.
I have been to the lowest,
most pathetic sink of
despair,
and I have jumped from
cushion to cushion
flying in an ecstatic reverie,
glorious.
When I throw my clothes
(like shackles aren't they?)
to the floor my heels
depress themselves slightly
sighing in released tension

like stripped tree limbs
in fall.
Barren and sheared
scrubbed of everything
unclean
in my eyes,
I can exist side by side
to the swinging of
my organs,
leaving me optimistic in
the sense that
for now
at least
I'm free from something.

rock

it's four in the morning
going on noon
as I'm rocking and rolling
unafraid of trivialities like
darkness and depth
the loom on both sides of
the sheetrock
cutting
grinding
rocking
rolling
and I'm excited
about what I have to say
until reprimanded
at which point I revert back

to a prearranged idyllic state in which
I am the ultimate in humility
and progression
for a good five minutes
till I have something wondrous to say
honestly believing that my words are
a furturistic mold of comprehension
raw and inadequately faceted
the base being the murky tasks
cheekily grinning from the tree limbs and
disappearing with petulant snorts and
the waving of their bushy tails.
every way I succeed as a man today
is based on the lie of a line
grotesquely fat and futilely stretching
with wide, crumbling sides
the monstrous soul of which
absolutely teems with polarities
of pleasure and the unutterable
debasement of the majority that is
valuable and worthwhile.
for an hour
hopefully
I can ride a fledgling gray goose
feeling like I'm riding the rails
of the migration to subjectivity
toward everything I've been
so incapable of settling.

Leroy is the gatekeeper
he always succeeds
claiming victory
to remind me
over and over
amidst the growing gloom
that
the crash
approaches like the Midnight Express coming

home again to the same location
the same 'place'.
And so it's four-thirty in the morning
and I have appointments to keep
with the convent
but I'm still rocking
rolling
consuming my whole through
sheer enjoyment, utter satisfaction
and the flawless confidence in
the flip of the coin twisting in the
air above
these trembling hands.

optimistique

dreading the day like
threading a needle
breeds a subliminal source code of
consummation and
needs.
the sun will rise and
the fog will dissipate under the
calm wrath of the baby blue
bath coating the space between
raindrops,
we all will awake inside of our
Rorschach minds or
roll over and peel our eyes from
the imperfections of the wall
to discover that it is
finally morning and that

indeed
the sun *is* rising,
and as babies are born to breed
and start to die,
i bow to a redemptive musing
and rise in the morning
throwing my wrists and dancing,
my thoughts not concentrated
on the upcoming day,
but rather,
the day after and the past success
ravenously scoured from the
wreck of yesterday.

you're not the only one

i will not last much longer here
this memory is depreciative
and dissociated
i have to salvage a lasting peace
with these blue roses and
hydrangeas
"light a candle" i whispered
chuckling
"this hurts me more than it
hurts you"
i locked the door.
next to the mailbox a man
patiently waits in flannel knickers.
the neighbors across the street
are watching a movie
the children curled up at the feet

of the couch
helpless blue halos hanging limp over
their fallen heads.
standing in the hall i feel a breeze
but the windows are closed.
the computer screen flashes no line
over and over again.
i open the door to the moon howling
lonely without his old friend.
cats are fighting in the alley.

this is a foreign house on foreign soil
adrift on a greased hot-plate
there is no messiah for this *choza*
facing a trial by fire.
an oppressive stench pierces my nostrils
and quickly
my tattered jeans are spattered.
from deep within a trance i emerge
docile as ever.
the night is warm and bright
disrupted only by the distant wail of
sirens and the flapping of sandals
swiftly pounding on the
cracked pavement.

big mouth, big page

I'm staring at a blank page,
like I'm sure we've all
done before,
thinking about the viability of

creative literature as a
profession,
in all honesty, the writers
we so adore have
simply sublimated and
adjusted their focus
according to a pale vacuum
that fills the hollow
deep in the center of
balance with
chaos and varying uncertainty.
Can you imagine?
Before I reflect and assess,
I am taken with the words
that flow down the
left side of the page
like ants caught in a rain gutter,
crawling and creeping
over each other in order to benefit
the whole, yet insatiably
striving to remain alive.
That's what I tell myself.
The real writers I know
are mostly aware of
the fact that they are caught up
in the act of exploiting
others with the
messiness of bitterness,
caught watching their words flow
down cheeks and onto pages
that capture the tenacity, pride and
power inherent in the
continuation of life.
I live, so far as I am aware,
as does everyone else, and take
a good deal of my motivation
from the very fact that I can
still fuck

get out of bed most mornings
and work till my hands bleed
towards the completion of a tangible
career, rather than this
vague poem that will always mean more
as a reflection, rather than
profit.
Maybe I'm just rationalizing
away the
lack
of talent that I cannot hurdle,
convincing myself that as I
cannot use what I love as a career,
at least it has saved my life,
that much more.

It's not so blank of a page now.

<u>wake up call</u>

I ride a two horse sleigh,
white, chipped paint and leather seat,
once a deep shade of brown, torn
neatly down the middle. She smiles,
looking up over the bright red scarf
snaked around her neck. I pretend I don't see,
so I can appear rugged, nonchalant,
stoic. A perfect profile shot.
Her cheek is resting on my arm,
her hands tucked deep inside my coat.
The wind blows snow in our faces,
clicking against our teeth and abruptly

cracking branches thickly piled with
a wool sweater of snow.
Neither of us knows where we are going,
an embellishment of the senseless nature of
anyone's destination.
We cross coated fields lined with rickety fences
and dotted with abandoned hay bails
and neglected machinery,
left to weather the storm as a monument
to spring. we pass through a small grove
oddly reeking of cedar, though no such
plant could grow in such a frosty breeze.
The sun emerges and shines straight unto
our upturned guises. The glory of the moment
overtook me, crashing through my bloodstream
as a rush of bulls engorged with adrenaline.
Such moments, however, bring to mind the
temporal vacuum of awareness, a misleading
notion confounding the intricate notion of
a lifetime.

I flick the reigns and stop the sled backwards at the edge
of the encroaching darkness, the wheels
resting resolutely at the edge of a small ravine.
As I jump off the bench I hear the crunch of her feet landing,
echoing off the naked trunks, kissing the iced glove holding
this diamond spattered snow globe.
Rounding the flank of my vaunted horse, still breathing
heavily, I see her, ensconced in light, making her shy eyes
shine in tacit kindness. I cross
the distance in one stride, raising my finger to her chin
and lifting her face into mine.
She grips my arms and pulls me tightly to her chest,
slipping through my hands and falling backwards
into the growing trench. I reach out in vain, her body
immaterializing in front of me, her wan smile fading
quickly into the air,
crackling with the hanging icicles.

The alarm goes off.

here is your poem.

i'm done
done with the nonplussed
the unaffected
your trivial comments bounce off
into the cavernous bowl of
a misappropriated multitude
like flies to a popping, crackling
shock therapy

you are nothing but a bane
a pittance of selflessness
a deception
you make claims based off of
the reactions figuring on the
various elements of my face
a shifting puzzle of disappointment
your bitterness
and the misconception that your time
in relation to a belated son of fire
is an efficient expenditure of time and
energy

i'm done
and now, with the thrashing churn of
a spontaneous appendectomy
picking apart my organs without heed
to order, function or form,
i can nonetheless rise from the floor
where my knees have sunk
like intertwined roots
into the carpeted floor beneath me.

the important thing is to keep

breathing.
keep walking
never stop walking
forwards, onwards
moving away from that place
that place in your head that is empty
cold, barren and devoid of any warmth
any type of desire to keep
this up
and
walk out that goddamn door
into the golden hope
inherent in sunshine,
one beautiful solitary finger held
resolutely in the air,
a phallic pillar of an adamant
defiance of the crashing sky,
the only thing left to say.

interviews

as a human I dream
when I sleep
but as an existential ghost
hovering outside of the apathetic shell
of an eggshell skull bounded
on all sides
by a thick, earthen coat of
autumn armor,
I cannot bring myself to
rise above the constraints of
this subjective and intersubjective,

contextual misunderstanding;
this reality.
the imagination flourishes in my
small death, much like the
fleeting reprieve of the climactic,
unbound of the strangling
interpretation that stifles the deep
resonation of my throat.

it is incredible how it piles on.

I had a dream last night that I shit my pants.
I woke up nervous, hesitant to move,
to reach down and discover an
all new form of humiliation.
rousing myself, dreading and pleading
I discovered that nothing was wrong.
my sphincter had come through,
so to speak.
it hit me then, a laughable backhand to
my cheek,
that I was still dreaming. my face,
hovering on it's own in the mirror,
spun in circles and, with eyes tinged with
crimson rings, laughed with a thick malaise.
I woke up, drenched in sweat,
amphibious. My hand
shot down through my
cold boxers
and stayed.

I just forgot
what town I am in
sitting haphazardly
half cocked
on an airport bar stool
does it even matter
which one
or are they all the same
relative to a final
destination not worth
leading up to
like beer before shots
before stories and hand shakes
arguments over tabs
women and politics
and the engines outside
in the smug heat
are warming up
as if ready
to forget where I am
too.

airport chalk talk

she fires from the
hip bang
I'm free
the Dementor has met
The Stag
and the bonds, the hazy
constraints of love
are torn asunder
and suddenly I can
smile
I can talk to them
and even
pinch an ass or two
or three.
we'll see
let this plane
fly on
34,000 feet
512 miles per hour
two new Peruvian friends
just shooting the shit
like cowboys
and hopping up and down
still holding the reigns
the wind bucking my sails
as if beckoning.
I know she is
cozy, already in the arms
of the next victim
and, as if tossed out
the emergency exit
depressurizing this cabin
my once irascible, tenacious

and all encompassing love
is turned inwards
radiating out in all directions
just another
ball of sunshine
supernovae event
melon balling
those pits of pain
that had once
defined me
yesterday.

Bang!

Cuzco

She slept in my arms
in that tiny hostel bed
for no apparent reason
other than to reverberate
heartbeats
for a moment.
Cocaine and booze
loose soles and shoes
left on the dance floor
wild dancing turned
vapid kissing
and now we are
there
snoring like the damned
while wishing the sun
would just pull in tune

to the stars crossed
and one very
broken guitar.

She had looked at me
earlier in that particular spin
asking why and how
goading me on
to Ecuador
to Colombia
to everywhere
leaving me as she slept
to wonder these very questions
aloud
in wonder.

I bought my tickets right then.

So we danced, later
carousing with no direction
knowing full well
the flight plans gone
orders of inoperations.
We smiled.
Lines disappeared.
When we returned
she held back, teasing
kissing and smiling
and then she was mine
cradled
and we slept a dream
much like waking
up to a raw
and seamless adventure.

what happened to carrier pigeons

she writes
and there it goes again
that damnable churning
percolating as if shaking
shaking as if percolating
and generally
just marshaling atoms into
synaptical warbling
very much like Machiavellian Morse Code
this time
it's a beach
there's a blonde from Holland
dominating my attention
there's a guy from my hometown
wanting to imbibe
and there she is
nothing but fermented mistakes
making me want to make
her
all over again.
How is it that we are so enchanted
as to punish ourselves
just a Rosicrucian fantasy
with Lucifer in the back seat
saying
Call her!
Trade me!
Drink this!
So I do, one very pale
logical fallacy
lost amongst
the salamander gone
misdirection oven

and here it comes
plastering over the holes
I created
leaving
the gradually sinking, slipping
serrating memories;
the unbearable lightness
of relearning to be alone.

familiar reductions

It's a miracle of transference
just an ocean
without a skipping stone
please make this stop
this relentless osmosis
pounding surf
and a heartbeat I sometimes
wish would just fade away
as if that little monkey
dropped the stick and cymbal
we're all just impermanence
personified
and they want me to get
counseling again
take the red pill
that will send me to a catatonic
stupor of ne'er do well
never worth writing about
how did I get here
how did it all come down
to one woman's

decision making process
guess im only flotSam
driftwood waiting to bleach
waiting to be deemed
however reluctantly
worthy of burning
throw dirt over shoulders
till there's a summit to bag
lighters to flick till there's
an inferno to ride down to the
depths of something tangible
and flap away till there's
wings to fly on
and the data
those 1's and 0's
keep scrambling on across
plastic windows
just another font dictating a race
not quite made of melanin
but ultimately porous
and absolutely worth transmitting
transferred
as small strokes
on a very small screen.

"I'd like to return this."

what a pity
I don't miss you now
that the entire thing was
nothing in the end
we were playing house

and the anxiety cast shadows
deep as eyes
we never really used
and we were so in love
when you straddled my chest
kissed my forehead
and whispered
it's going to be ok
but the jungle beckons
the bus is honking
and we are moving on
birds spraying red clefts
as they lift languorously
into the air, leaving nothing
just like trains
no, I don't miss you
but I remember
your face
your hands
the times you tried to be
anything but yourself
to be with me
and I will remember
and remember
then yet now
thinking that these
girls
buses
birds and
enveloping jungles
could easily replace you
and knowing
full well
that that
they
never will.

vaminos

trying to stay calm
when your heart throws
in the ventricle
you're on the way to an office
outside of the delirium tremors
induced haze, the bleary sunshine
and the tranquilly waving arms
of that goddamn plane
I better be on
in an hour or two
as he takes everything
tossing it to the side with
terse glances
and languid limbs
my mind races
another greyhound tearing off
for dinner
where the hell did I...
what was...
did it...
and we're all cool as cucumbers
just calmly sweating
a glowing artillery shell heart attack
bombarding
through choked pores
and its over
nope
you hand him your wallet
then it dawns
that one little thing
totally forgotten till
right
now

that rolled up sole
probably
definitely
frosted
he finds it immediately
eyes cast grimly on your
ever so suddenly
not entirely copacetic frame.
he holds it up to his nose,
questioning.
something in Spanish.

"No se?"

he holds it to his lips,
questioning
a hard look plastered
to a hardened face.
something in Spanish.
I can see small flakes
falling
down
to the
desk.
marijuana?

"No se?"

he shrugs. Vaminos.

"..."

VAMINOS!

vaminos
it is
and I
stagger

to the front
of the security line
shaking
hopefully imperceptibly
do they sell
beer
at ten
please sell beer
at ten
walking fast
poker face
on
shrugs
shrugs
shrugs
and I get on the
plane
feeling the last of the drip
the cute, busty flight attendant
winks
and
what the flying
fuck
just happened.

<u>flash friends</u>

Oh, hey brother
look at you look at all you've
become and been
and look at that hair...
and here you are

lines and letters
presumptive of a reality
in your face
beaming or snarling
depending on the eye level
of apathetic glee
you've chosen to imbibe with
today
good to see you
good to meet you
today
it's as if these events
scribed and unrolled
are the very dictation
of your particular place
amongst the stars.
Fuckin' groovy mate.

A word to the wise
watch your own hands sometime
brother
as you raise them from the sink
watching yourself as you fixed
that fucking hair!!
and think of all the tools you've held
the hair you've brushed back
behind her ears
the strings you've plucked
trying to sing and wail
trying to figure out
exactly the moment it all
went right or wrong.

Think of their smiles
the bathrooms you've stood in
one on your dick, one on the wall
brother
think of all the ropes, shovels

bed sheets and steering wheels
think of the rocks come loose
above you
think of the dirt chocked and stuffed
underneath your nubs of fingernails
then look up to your face
and try to befriend those eyes
yet again
as equals along a wide open plain
where the answer truly lies
in not giving one fuck
yet caring some about nothing
all the same
in the name of wildly gambling
on the craps game of animalhood.

Brother I may have never met you
and I may never hold you up
the sun rising
staggering away from concrete
realities
responsibilities
and, heaven forbid
cocoa butter stained change
yet I will share a double yellow or
white line
or two
for the moment long enough
to ease all of our reigns
if only
as a momentary lapse
amongst the inevitable strain
inherent
in realizing you're
here
for the time
being and
nice to fucking meet you.

operator

Well, here it is plain as paper
alone for the same reasons
in a very hot
yet somehow cold world
and new things
enthralling things
come and go
with the sun, the moon
the tide
drawing an unending
teeter totter session
between glee and joy
bitterness and grief
belly laughs and hellos
stuttered sobbing and goodbyes.

Why did you have to write?

This train was far away
churning through cities, hell bent
on destruction gone creation
a congenial back slap from
the demons hounding
while the angels guiding
squeeze my hands
so encouragingly.

Now it's a surf town
this chalk white gringo
crouched crab like in front
of the break, a stones throw
from bikinis, umbrellas and boards
resolute in nothing

but the status of my wallet.

Now she wants me to call
"about your stuff"
as if this was a perfectly good reason
not to burn it
like I want to
as if I could possibly not
despite knowing
that I will never see
her in person
ever again.

One can only imagine.

So here it is, plain as white bread
sour, tired, renewed, enlightened
hardened
and ready to lay my head down
and let the surf pound my
doubts back into minerals
as they belong
for reasons
only an illusory concept
such as time
can determine.

<u>realistically</u>

his heart must be still
pumping, although,

fashionably delayed and
with effect, I'm sure,
the big ticker
has stopped making noise, has
stopped leading.
in life, with all of the miscellany,
melodrama and shit shows,
baring chest outwards
onwards, as they say
becomes integral yet intangible,
none the less crucial
in order to retain a shred of
idealism, of how things should be.
it's funny that most of maturity lies
in the difference between prudence
and pragmatism,
realism just the foot stamp on your back
you, with your childish bleeding heart,
still squatting atop
the red square,
you have lost, somehow, something
along the way
fell out of the engine,
stopping you dead in your tracks
as the blood pours from your hands
and the small, red Buddha figurine
held for so long by scarred and crippled fingers,
drops to the ground and bounces,
only to fall again and jump around,
finally ending on its side,
comatose yet insistently
twinkling on the pavement.

It was around the second
Jackie Chan movie
that his head began to shrink
to a size significantly smaller
than his father's
yes
it was there
somewhere
deep in a bejungled countryside
astraddle a window
creating a universal portal with
aviation shades
that he came to the writing
in the clouds, the trees, the kisses
Hello
he said, smiling
I have been long enough
haven't I?

missed

it's been damn near a month
and this hasn't faded
a bit
Ed Sheeren, you fuck
in this rainy, fronded
escape from settled
a middle of somewhere
the chaff and debris
cast in wakes lobbed upwards
like that of a very specific shuttle
that shed skin and shuddered
on reentry
once was enough
and now
past the spite and malice
mask of a face
ahead of a brain
that knows
while it may be all my fault
or hers
it may have been an ante-less
game you could have been
playing a majestic con
who knows
the fact remains
it's been a month
and I still love you
as if none of this had
ever happened
yesterday

groomed

you never know
till you do
another wasted
'wasted mid-20s'
cast like badly tied flies into
a burbling river
of poor decisions
great decisions
can't really tell
between those
and
long, broke trails
and an underlying knowledge
that despite a career deferred
the pursuit
was the only necessary
timecard
aside from temporarily bloated
accounts ready to spill.

This watershed, this confluence
of travelers finding and striving
determines nothing
yet somehow means everything
in the sense of
who do you want in charge?
What kind of blasphemous underwriter
to a corrupted constitution
of laws, loans, and shopping malls
do we need more than ever?
And who is it really,
a stones throw away
from your tacit cairn

that knows
the conglomerated truths
inherent in walking exactly the paths
they
pointed away from
when they were too old
to find out where they
lead?

it's gonna follow you anyway

head aching
the thought of her
coming through
despite the frenetic
pace I try
to drown it in
and I know, I know
I know so many things
just another loner
with a broken interior
a drinking issue
and a very quickly
ticking clock
well, hello Bogota
this is me at the end
broke and wondering
just what it's going to
take
to dig out of this hole
this time
just how long exactly

till this pen catches fire
till my mother
smiles when I tell her
where I am
when my brother returns
my calls
and maybe something really
is wrong
with me
it's cute
they think
that I have no self-esteem
but that exactly
couldn't be farther
from what
they think
is the truth
that being that I just
have a very firm
understanding of what
exactly
it is
that I
am.
so double knot them
my
insides, get it together
duct tape if you
have to
as I spray mucus in all
directions at least
the pain receptors
still work
so here it is
the next beer, line
recklessly intaken
head aching
in a country I never thought

I'd ever be
the thought of her
pervading the thoughts of me
and the ego gone confidence
gone to confidence
and an overblown ego
and I know
I am free
I know
all of the great things
wonderful things
somebody I won't remember
is saying to me
I know this will pass
but for now
the thought of her
coming through
is too dehydrated
to wash out
this alone
and waiting to blossom
into something egoless
in the new home
without that particular
her
oh yeah
I know
but just exactly
what that means
is harder to drown
out appropriately
with such short walks
and such
weak beer.

5 hours, 42 minutes

A child's feet in my back
and a loud, effeminate
flight attendant unnecessarily
buzzing at my elbow
just this particular continent's
means of nuisances
making me a patriot
as if I
never changed
so these travels
come and go
testing and retesting
reminding you just what
it was
that wasn't so bad
wasn't so crazy
and what was
actually worth leaving
in the first place.

There truly are glories
beyond the ephemeral blue
and this world
has beautiful women
who are anything but
American
still
there are the exigent
benefits of home
I may be blind to
often
but hurry back to
quickly

breathing deeply
and trying not to
get arrested
for assault
on creeps and children
alike
and as I remember
the miraculous highs
the nearly breathtaking lows
I smile
knowing that while some
have fooled themselves
into idiotic fantasies of
expatriotism
I return to the country
printed on this blue ticket
the lego and candy battleground
to wreak havoc
gleefully manipulate
and ultimately
thrive
in a sliding pinnacle
without a care in the
world
aside from how much longer
it'll take
to get
home.

You
won't
find
her

here.

for the sake of clams

I can tell she is getting angry
by how fast her beer is disappearing
she's using her hands now
snobby New York socialite
gone oil slicked Italian
and here come the names
and here comes the vitriol
just pent up anger from
another dehydrated soul
perforated to pieces with gnawed edges
somehow non affiliated
with how little I care.

"...and you pretend as if this is
a joke, is this a JOKE..."

and suddenly I'm back
the smell, the *feel* of sickness...
coating my veins, eyes and pores...
those greasy white walls
the spatters of my blood
circled by throngs of cockroaches
looking down to see the IVs attached
to my arms...

she's obviously drunk
off beer, vodka, or semblances of power
is anyone's guess
and as her glass drains
all I can see is the spoiled 13 year old
one hand on the gilded record player
the other white knuckling the door
ready to slam away

all of those untidy memories
decanted remonstrances
and the unchecked yearning gone bitterness
that permeates every word.

"...you look like a TOOL, like a PUNK,
like someone who never thought
to GROW UP..."

and the IVs shadow on the wall
played tricks and hell
as my vision shifted and suddenly
my things were there, the blood gone
and the nurse was spoon-feeding me
whispering in Spanish
smiling although I knew she knew
I was dying, supposed to be gone

I knew she had made that soup.

And good god, is she still yelling
yup, still screaming
something about a livelihood
responsibility, ultimately nothing
but a discordant and forgotten harmony
that I immediately knew
I wouldn't be around to watch
conducted.

"...YOU SEEM LIKE AN IDIO..."

Still talking.

"Just LEAVE. You're FRUSTRATING me!!"

U mad, brah?

I needed a cigarette

and I saw an air bubble
slowly making its way down
the tube to my veins
so I ripped them out
wobbling as I stood up
finding out later it had been days
walking out the front door
to the screams in Spanish
and lighting up
just as the nurse I am
not sure existed
on this plane
hopped into a moto taxi
coquettishly blinking and waving
all of those nurturing fingers
independent
then and there
I decided
no more 'bad days'
no more 'for granted'
and definitely never
to let another angel
fly away on a moto taxi
unencumbered.

And I return the next day
for money, of course
tight lipped with a mask of ignorance
knowing full well
how to charm a snake
you can tell she's still angry
irrationally so

"...well I'm sorry to see you go..."

but it's no use to poke
to prod
to cajole

sometimes you just have to
wad up the cash
and head for the door

"...good luck to..."

lighting up a cigarette
as you make tracks
and wondering, ever fucking wondering
where it all went wrong
and just how much
of it all
was real.

to Colorado

Tears welling
as the bus pulls out
just another failed experiment
the cartographer's pen dripping
with piss, blood and vinegar
sighs unfolding over the beer
soaked map
he outlined my current life on
it felt like home for a minute
till they all started talking
and one day the ax fell
they wanted (needed really)
someone to be
something I am not
so here are the half-hearted
goodbyes and terse glances

here are the ditches, the barren highways
that have come to define me
and there goes an aging manchild
looking for the next set of swings
the next impenetrable little town
the next dusty page
to write
shitty prose on
as the water recedes
the airport, my hotel
looms
and this square, aluminum worm
chugs on
carrying one heinously broke storyteller
looking for a home more permanent
than a three hour bus ride
to Boston.

submitted

And the spark comes back
with a flash
like something that never left
dragging its nails across your face
and screaming please don't shut the
door
don't shut me
out
Sam
please don't
leave
and here's another panel truck bar

here's another time when I should be
sleeping
spending money and time wisely
instead of pissing it down my own
throat
alone this bristly Friday night
entertained by only my flying thumbs
well,
welcome back inspiration
it's good to have someone to drink
with again
I know you can hear me hear them
the paranoid delusions
we share
as if we've done something
wrong
or sinister
aside from taking up molecular frequency
or simply being
tired and alive.

keep looking up

from the ground your head never seems
quite as big. it is clear,
from this particular vantage point,
that you've fucked up. next
the blows, the triple entendre of
ringing ears, swollen jaw and
the myriad of colored streams,
stars blasting in through the edges of
your eyes,

the prophet of humility,
blatantly brute in a white smoking jacket.

if it mattered who's hand was grinding
my face into the pavement,
a picture resembling a pancake being
squashed into the pan, burning,
it would be my old friend.
the fact that one is lost, wandering in their
own morality, their own viable
alternatives, their own casual blend
of emotional turbulence and snack trays of
material alternatives,
says to me that it might as well be,
potential crashing over faint constraints of mind,
the man who sleeps in my house
that stands above me and
laughs with his cadre of
bobble-heads.

there is always a day you will lose.
despite your best attempts,
you will break, and you will have to face the
grim consequences of what your life
has manifested.
that day, I had led with avarice and returned
with shame, burning hot from my
fried face.
they say fool me once
shame on you.
fool me twice?
well you ain't going to fool me twice.

I've always known
I'll try anything twice and
granted
that I'm a mistake addict,
I can safely assume that

I'll be there again
in that
particular vantage point
but it doesn't
bother me in the least.
how else can
one
practice the stubbornness and
needless defiance
that as symbols of the apathetic
generation
think astride the arms of sofas
and live for?

trying to shake my boots

The stress seeps in like rain through a shotgunned rain coat
finding every crack and crevice to slowly creep through
in order to link arms in brotherly camaraderie with those
molecules
of water that I consider to be mine and only mine. For the next
two days or so.
My heart is held in two trembling hands, adrenaline
seemingly
silhouetting the fragile frame and the BOM BOM of the beat
causing all kinds of traffic jams in the arterial highways
coursing
through my body at break break break break break break
neck speed.

I guess I should be doing something today but half assedly
searching

for new jobs, chord progressions, lyrics, classes, escape routes and,
of course, the next round of failed relationships of all kinds,
is taking precedence as the primary means of time recycling
gone wasting
that my viewers have come to expect from such a maladaptive
program.

And the anxiety keeps falling, beating against the ancient
window panes,
suddenly i'm outside trudging through the literal and
figurative ice floes
the glossed sheen of which crunches beneath my dollar store
shoes
in muted groans of pain, apathy and strong yet dispassionate
surprise.
There is the best burrito in my future but I simply cannot
make myself
positive and keen and everyone in the slam packed restaurant
is talking about
that weird guy on the corner of the bar quickly drinking a
Pacifico
whose leg is humming and whose face cannot settle on an
expression
appropriate enough for routine and mundane human
interaction.
So much for getting laid tonight.

The remedies have all been tried. No booze or weed, easy on
the cigarettes
just one cup of coffee and a solid work out regimen
interspersed with singing
dancing, strumming and tap tap tap tap tap tap tap tap on the
keys balanced
ever so stoutly over my crotchial region. My phone chirps
every hour or so,
just those fishing lines left to trawl behind the boat in a half
hearted and

full-balled attempt to get my dick into a still-breathing female
and I cannot for the life of me figure out how to make a bank
account big enough
to get it all done, get some traction and make something hap
hap hap hap happen.

They tell me I need to get help as they have always told me to
get help but the real
question is what the living hell the definition of 'help' is when
I can't even define
exactly what it is the 'problem' is or exactly why it is that I
have been perpetually
sidelined in the face of those dance routine addled teenage
and early adulthood
activities, memories and group activities that we are all
supposed to have out of
an attempt to maintain some semblance of a tradition-based
cultural experience
that no one is actually ever a real part of.

It must have been the girl.
It's always the girl. I was doing great and then I met
another one who immediately proceeded to give me a stellar
chance with, a series
of events that I then followed, ten seconds later, with the coup
de grace.
I actually asked her if...
Maybe I don't need to go over
that again.
The pillar I put her on, the slow decline, the ever widening
hole
inside and out, the disillusioned conceptions of how to get the
hell out of here
wherever here is and there is a question lingering over this
Mexican food
and this bottle and this block set as a fence alongside the main
boulevards
and the breaks nonexistent in this rusted city that I kicked her

out of
with all of my money in her pocket and the carefully crafted
persona I can't
see in the mirror in her mind but this is not about her, I think
this is about the stress creeping in like rain though coats
blasted with flak cannons
and ordained as the savior of everything dry and untainted,
of everything these molecules would strive to teach outside of
this citadel of rain
and this bodice left taut and bound to the beatings of a heart
one rant away from bursting.

as I look onto a new
sheet of paper
imaginary in the literary
sense
yet so impressingly
apparent in appearance
I find that the
words pressing my tongue
behind the lock
tied bag of
standoffishness
throughout the evening
float through the crevices
between my teeth,
pushed benignly
to the side
by the readiness to cast truth
into open waters
for a more
acceptable portrayal
than these
silly words
fished across
imaginary paper.

in the bucket

there's a hole
somewhere inside of me
where the rain used to soak in
that now just pours with a hope
for snow
for tables
for anything worth building on
as the days slip by
and nowhere
seems to be the only place
that I know well
hey there old friends
how've you been
as we haven't been talking
i've made others
since you last
stayed there
but still
it's never been the same
and now I get to learn it all over
holding the hand of a dream
showing her the ropes
of a life I fucked up
the last time
I
waited in line
and she has so much potential
just as life has every ability to
kick you down
to the grave
and yet, I can't help but feel the pangs
of what if

if I had been able to conquer
the silly maladaptions
and yet this hole keeps leaking
they tell me
I need some help
and who knows
if that man agrees
but still
kick your damn feet up and watch the show
here's a check
here's my life story
for you to tell your goddamn wife
as mine just tries to get old enough
to be so
observe this page ripping
against a goddamn soul
they think is weak
enough to bustle
I just never was cowardly enough
to shut down,
never scared enough
not to say it all,
never weak enough to die.

And they think that I am flimsy.

I have walked through more streets
alone than most people
have walked in their entire lives
I remember what it was like to relish
simply having a friend
any friend
to share the road with
till I realized
that they had loved me the entire time
I had just hated them so strongly
that they had forgotten
ever as quickly

as a goldfish finding food
and now they have no choice but to
recognize
the person bathed and armored
in an insanity bred from
loneliness, self-imposed genius,
and too many pulled triggers
to ever work in an office
or pretend as if this life was worth
pretending to be human for.

See, there's a hole somewhere in my chest
where the rain will always pour through,
because I can't run,
from where I am from,
from where my first words hit paper,
from where I ruined it all
time and again.

I cannot help but remember where
that hell resides that
I can't admit to,
every word I write
scratching at the surface
as if that sentence soothes a burn
as the rest of the page
is slowly burning me alive.

Hey shrink.
How much time do you got?

pay no mind

a mind is a
peculiar entity, as placement into
the ephemeral constraints
of words would be
to simply confuse itself.
trenchant in organization,
reflective due to the
glassy Formica shield
bristling under the heat
simmering beneath,
the synaptic interdependent
communication network
dictating the pace
of your adaptation
is ever reminded of the.
the, the practical extension
of the senses into a tangible,
feasible, modicum of expression.
it becomes imperative, in light
of the futility inherent in
hurry, to question the bounds
of environment, of 'the'
the current constituency of
which
enchants the network into
revealing
neuroticism, liberality and
biased rationality, then stemming
from a manner of existence
incongruous to the preconstituted
dialectic echoing between
the looming towers of western culture,
intimidating from your
perch on the musty ground of
main street
just a mind driving a rotting bag
looking inwards at itself

as it feels the outside and ultimately
pays no mind
to a particular either
or aether
subjected to the subjection of such a
peculiar entity.

Jimbo's 100th

Dripping in the wet heat
near the beach where he had made his home
I follow a shamelessly crusted blue scooter
putt-putting its way up the slight incline
the thin wisps of smoke churning
over the battered hood of my car.

Jimmy is dancing, as best he can,
kicking his legs and pointing at
any passerby quick enough to look up
in time.
He is high on life, jubilant for the future and yes,
he's still drunk.

Because this is Jimmy's 100th time to rehab,
that invariable process of drying out,
of coming to terms with the oppressive weight
of piggy-backing way too many demons to
the gates and back.
Despite the obvious concerns and immortal
processes inherent in killing one's self via
that one particular organ
there are many who see this as the veritable

Golden Battlefield for ascendance.

There are those that see it as the only way
out of here.

I shared Jimmy's 100ᵗʰ last drink.
I was there for the 100ᵗʰ final countdown.
I will most likely not be there
for the 101ˢᵗ.

I remember sitting underneath
the muggy January clouds
the pine trees flapping contentedly
and the skeleton restaurant crew
howling toward a sly island fever
via the previously full half gallon.
I remember Jimmy trying bravely
to hold back the tears, the flood
of death and heartbreak
forcing out through the pores of
least resistance
despite his obvious mastery of such
contrivances.
I remember him telling me that
that particular bottle
would invariably be the end of him.

Purely in the metaphysical sense.

Now, outside of the cookie cutter
facility scattered across a cement field
baking underneath a hesitant sun
I shake Jimmy's shaking hand
laughing as you can only laugh
when there is absolutely nothing else
left to do
as Jimmy will be a friend of mine
till he is claimed with the recycling

dried out and poured
into a dirt cocktail
till he finds his way
following those of us along the path
out of here
the end of what
yet to be determined
is as humid as the Florida haze
ultimately just a pine-scented reverie
in the car ride of this immediacy
that Jimmy and those others
with two legs
find themselves saying
goodbye to at least
100 times a day.

curriculum vitae

i cut the umbilical cord
years ago from the womb of
expectation and societal understanding.
whether i am talented or not,
whether i will fit between the brackets,
the book ends,
the rubric of general society,
is beyond me.
for now i live on the rails; in between the
only lines i will ever define myself by:
those striped white and yellow lines
that direct the channel of metallic
salmon stoically struggling

upstream to an impending doom.

i write.
i put words on the screen,
the backs of receipts,
bus tickets and
tattered notebooks till
my eyes stop opening.
even then i ghost write
from the aether, churning through
words as if holding back the tide
enveloping the pragmatic minds of
those in the center stream.

this
is not how things need to be
so i plan to find
just how things
should.
until then these words will stream
from my fingers like rhetoric
from the masks of the politicians
you revere.
until then, i still hold the scalpel
above the page,
slicing in to the organs of this
misappropriated culture we have spawned
as larvae onto the fragile soil beneath
aching knees.

as i drift, aimless and pointless,
for reasons that won't exist in
each passing second,
i will continue to hack away
at the catatonic attitude
surrounding the minds of
you and yours.
advice is for those that truly

don't understand.
understanding is for those who readilly
don't act.

the middle ground is the
unpromised land
and it is guarded by razor wire
made of umbilical cords
and doubt, wildly tossed boulders
and bordered, of course, by a cadre
of words jettisoned out assholes
by those that resemble
those remarks
just letters turned to sentences
turned to flaking scales
pushed up current in a frantic
attempt to fuck or
write
before it all comes to a
crashing, churning, flooding
halt.

23rd

it's a sign of
resilience
to maintain the same
forces of habits
that have propelled
you through
so many identicals
and days

in so many words.

it's a beautiful
bright and burgeoning
day and again
I sit
sunburned and grimacing
as the bouncing
skirts and thighs
tribulate so happily
in eddies around my
sidewalk table.

the words pouring
from my pen have
no recourse,
naturally,
against the imminent
realization that with
a gift comes
some barren form of
deficiency.

I only ever
wanted
to get laid.

funny how this
shit
usually works out
huh?

ringing

So here it is again
another pang of loneliness
Tinseltown of dead Christmas trees
and violently reverberating memories
shes gone and
she hates me and
she loves me and
shes sorry
and there are still no friends,
the issues are still clinging to my chest
as soul-sucking leeches
and the microscope is against my forehead
looking in and in and in and in
and telling me nothing I want to hear
nor anything i'm capable of handling
or remedying
just quite yet.
Get help they say,
go talk to someone
so I find this keyboard
and I stare at the leaking ceiling
and I think about the rest of her things
that I have to mail to her mother's house
and I look at the blood marks on the carpet
and the tattered paint still holding on
to the door frame
and I want to fade again
just run away
give up
let the myriad of mistakes and fuck ups
that has shaped my life
just explode in a dizzying array of tears

and then quickly ebb and fizzle
on the next available tide.

The pangs become a dull ache
and I still can't sleep in the bed
the couch swallows me for days
and the phone tweets and twitters
just a red canary quietly and urgently
letting me know
that she is still thinking about me
and how am I doing?
How am I feeling?
How about I turn the damn thing off
cut her out like the corners of a paper snow flake
and then burn the fuckers as they swish
back and forth
to the wet grass beneath my porch
as if its happened 1000 times
and the whiskey coursing its way through
your veins and brains and balls
keeps you grounded at one electron higher
than the floor your feet are slipping off
the rails creak and shake
and the whole damn world just goes about
its own damn business, giving no shit
about just another mess
not worth cleaning up
drooling and fuming
over the blood stained and shattered pane
thoughts of you.

ER

What they don't understand
is that I'm fighting myself
more than anything else
with just two balls and
nowhere to go
I can't find a breath
I can't find a means
I can't find a goddamn thing
worth doing either for
they just laugh and enjoy
rinse, repeat
hand me that goddamn bottle
before I steal it, down it
and pop you with it
I just don't know why I was
ever spawned
who thought that
this
would be just a grand idea
just two parents popping out
something they can't be bothered to ignore
like it's their job
so they can have the satisfaction
of looking at who I made myself into
of the ways that I painstakingly
carved their flaws from my bloodstream
of the words I say from a
mind still pounding as if swollen
as if beaten to a bloody pulp by its innards
as if hemorrhaging.

triple s and an enema please

I shaved my pubes today.

It's a modern world.
We write about concepts
that have already been derived
and deriven
so many words
put in so many different ways
and still the goddamn same
so yes,
I shaved my pubes today.

There are cuts and nicks
chaff turned to nuisances
scattered across the barren
plain of shower that
I share
with the rest of this microbial
plane.

It looks like a three year old
just went at an afro
with a weed whacker
and I am laughing
along
as if it is some grand joke
that we all try so damn hard
to be these immaculate representations
of something we can
never hope to achieve.

It looks like I tried to care

more than anyone
just jumping in line for
the parade
waving a sparkler and sporting
an American Flag button-up
made in Bangladesh
and yelling at the top of my lungs
"I PLEDGE ALLEGIANCE!"
to what is unclear
to the screen based communication
to the routine strivations
to the understanding that an SUV
always trumps a dark bar, that
these beautiful women
need to be paid for
to the apathetic indignation framing
a set of opinions and ideals
everyone shares about love and war
yet no one has the balls to do anything
about.
That flag. This country. I love them both
in the context of small towns, of those
rare forms of light that emanate
from even rarer people
I pledge allegiance to the customary,
not the contemporary, those muskets
that drew blood, that carved out a piece
are long buried and replaced with
reality TV, strip malls, production and
commercialistic porn
just a haircut away
from gleefully acquiescing to
see,
I shaved my pubes today
according to the wishes of a woman
slowly, and ever so surreptitiously,
trying to mold me into the statue
that derived essence

of man,
of country,
of an evolved
societally based
solipsism
inherent in a modern world
just waiting for a cut and shave
a wash and wax and wane
and one man to get with the
program
as he realizes
one hair at a time
what a fool he's been.

I was listening

my life is as different
as anyone but that
fortunately
is negligible
given the option I will pull the yoke
into the tracks pacing this
shit stained highway and
tear off
across the dirty alleys
without hesitation
without a blink or shudder
I would drop this placid
situation
drawing in with a droning osmosis
a slow current towards
the painfully regular

I don't have the option of hope
anymore
some god of something decided
to aim the shit-cannon
directly at my back and
fire in the hole
we're all in the same game,
but the rules do not follow
the hollow tenets we have come
to embrace by taking for
granted that
sarcasm is a shitty bandaid and
in the morning I get up with a smile
because
if not, I will sink back under the sheets
and suffocate in what will
probably
and what won't
subsequently
become something
altogether more tangible
than a life different
in every facet
and as negligible
as you said it'd be.

snooze buttons

as a human I dream
when I sleep
but as an existential ghost
hovering outside of an apathetic shell

of an eggshell skull bounded
on all sides
by a thick, earthen coat of
autumn armor
I cannot bring myself to
rise above the constraints of
this subjective, inflective
contextual misunderstanding;
this reality.
the imagination flourishes in my
small death, much like the
fleeting reprieve of the climactic
unbound of the strangling
interpretation that stifles the deep
resonation of my throat.

it is incredible how it piles on.

I had a dream last night that I shit my pants.

I woke up nervous, hesitant to move,
to reach down and discover an
all new form of humiliation
rousing myself, dreading and pleading
I discovered that nothing was wrong
my sphincter had come through
so to speak.

it hit me then, a laughable backhand to
my cheek
that I was still dreaming. my face
hovering on it's own in the mirror
spun in circles and, with eyes tinged with
red rings, laughing with a thick malaise
I woke up, drenched in sweat
amphibious. My hand
shot down through my
cold boxers

and stayed.

reentry

the bird I flew
broke apart on reentry
scattering my premonitions and memories
across the universe
and
ultimately rending the fabric
of homeostasis asunder in a spectacular
display of physics versus time

as I tumbled,
careening out of control in ecclesiastic spirals,
my rendition of an evasive maneuver,
I couldn't help but scream an
ecstatic bellow
of so much goddamn rage against
the pretenses that had led to
such a misappropriation of life and talent
as the world came
ever closer
the nausea that was filling my helmet with
bile, vomit and bitters
subsided and became a
a memory of reconstitution

then my liver exploded and my own hell
broke loose
confetti erupting in a cloud resembling the
electrons around an atom
my heart stopped several times, hesitating
a toilet half-assedly plugged
internally catastrophic and cauterized
by the very thing

melting the barriers of a once efficient
light show

and the ground crept closer, waving arms
ready to catch my frame and embrace
the feathers caught on thermals above
a howling rend in the stratospheric fabric
not sturdy enough to maintain
the weight of such a homeostasis
ten seconds away from
splatting across a page
looking an awful lot
like the ground.

such an asshole

oh,
is it pleasant to
discover
the basic prevalences of personality
that dictate the outward behavior
perceived by the irresolute
masses that you
stroll right by
evidence that has
quite literally
been spinning before the
crook of your nose
suddenly
becomes the blatant truth
beckoning the verisimilitudes
that pervade your mind like

locusts.

oh,
is it great to be
such an asshole,
as to confuse even
ones self in such paradoxical
mental meanderings
when the sneer
turns to a fist
through the wall
in rehab they told me
my days of
getting angry
were over
a new dawn was rising in the
face of recovery
worth telling the world about

that's what they called it,
recovery.

oh,
how could anyone have guessed,
that a reconstitution would
lead to so much
back tracking
now that i've escaped the
clutches of those
that implant their own
ideals and notions of verisimilitude
into the folds of
those too young to
know better
I have found that
the pungent stench
burning under my
scathing nostrils

is the remnants of a
lifetime of
hatred and bitterness
unexpressed
the basic tenancies
paying rent to a predilected rage
a genetic suitcase cuffed to wrists
swinging behind every dumpster
those incapacities drilled
onto flatboard, onto prefabricated
hulls and keels
adrift on a sea of outward demonstrations
finding out
via the tide
just what it was
that pissed me off
so much
in the first place.

saying something

We all talk without blinking
speaking of casual references
inferences and the happenstance dominating
the very breaths we vehemently snatch
amidst lies and choking laughter.
Even to the pages we dump our mindsets upon
so easily
we are nothing but the catch in a conversation
caught between idiosyncrasies
laced between thick leather bootstraps
and bombarded with synaptic neutrinos

cast from the flickering fusion
of our softly blazing retinas.

We weren't born dying.
It slipped into our lungs on the breeze,
a cloud of poisonous words,
a superlative, masochistic disease
that crept, node by node,
into the deepest recesses of spattered minds.
We began to die the day we chose,
the choice painfully possessive,
to take ourselves seriously.

We're only lost when there's nothing left to find.

I used to care about that incessant clamorings of my
misused form, worrying that
it was bad for me. That I wouldn't live as long.
(Hand me that bowl.)
There was a point where I realized
that what I was waiting for will never
ever come,
goals, the silly notion!, are simply a means
of organizing dead time.
What do you want to be
when you give up?
God doesn't love you,
we are alone on a pathetically cold rock,
swimming and stumbling,
scowling and sneering.
(Here, I'll pack one.)
So blast this music, this entrenched rhetoric
deep into your skull,
shake up the synapses,
maybe that will release enough
of those fucking chemicals
given to us through an umbilical cord
then sucked out through eyes, through teeth,

through the crook in our backs
that bends us over
so we can be fucked again and again in the
search of some time
of vain hope to propel,
of emotional propane.
(Hand me a beer.)

It's easy to see
as if it was ever hidden
in the light of what they call day
the incongruous lines
bracing the frame of what they call
experience
something becks and calls
to you, to it, to us
like a dog frantically straining
at the limit of the choke chain,
froth spewing out in a wild attempt
to fight, fly or die.

The truth, if such a loftily held concept
ever truly existed, consists of a variety
of underhanded deals, smirks and openly
held scorn; vitriol for those who simply
need someone to hate
the mind of whom
is crafty and ingeniously malleable,
two 'facts' that allow one, who is of such a
mind, to blend the myriad of perforated
realities into a palatable stew.

This by no means makes this
tolerable.

After the first six-pack the air becomes caustic
tearing at the linings of lung and esophagus
like draino tearing through the remnants of

beard and tooth decay. After the second
the very world itself becomes a barrier
hindering any attempt at transference
and we want, we need
another to chase it down.

we've been down so long,
so deep, the sinewy water
glassy in the bright summer sun,
seems like electric wire.
all we want, a very
complicated notion,
is a bright white life preserver
a rope from the 6th dimension,
some ladder or beanstalk
to climb in the hopes of finding the scalpel
necessary to remove the need
pressing behind
such fiery retinas.

Communication, this
game of wills, trying to
be the amusement they all
have come to count on,
while holding back the flood
of bitter disappointment
coursing like venom through a
channel of veins which will,
no doubt, soon run
smack dab
into our minds
is
to the man, the woman
the beasts
the grains of sand
marching on
as if unperturbed
with all of the nonsense

swirling around
on breezes cast by
drooping mouths
here the slithering smoke
drapes around the edge
of the screen and walls
as uncertain lights
flitter and flutter by
in wrist-swinging bliss
dictated in the archaic language
of everything we try to say
without speaking
blinking
or whipping out;
those elements dumped on the
seemingly real pages
in the hopes of saying something
really worth saying
or reading.

terminal velocity

while it has become
so readily apparent that
I
amongst others
am the current epitome
of solitude
it has occurred to me
ever so gradually
that this is how

I was born to be.

take this with a few
grains of salt.
or an ocean.
or vodka
and grapefruit.

breath in, breath out
and sleep
sleep
sleep away the
false memories and hopes of revival.

then run and gun
your way to a
quote/un-quote
better life.

if I was a better man
and this were a better world,
as it were,
I might have transpired and
waxed poetic on the relationships
I have tendered in my time
here
but this was not meant to be.
rather,
I have ruminated on the
blissful nostalgia that is
the fate
of such a solicitous endeavor
such as this.

what I have found
amongst the tattered remnants
of memory
has only served to bolster

the pretenses and notions
that have led to my
societal demise.

i'm still breathing,
I think
and falling has never
felt so good.

Missoula

Zip.
Click.

each step is harder
every mile like stretching
wings bent on breaking
this rope will snap
this man will break

Tick.
Tock.

give me a mountain to climb
rocks chalked and battered
something to conquer
give my fists and elbows some calcium
let me fight Tyson
can't hear a damn thing
over choked sobs
anyway

"Hey man, you alright?"

Click.
Click.
Yes.

faces appear
a crumbling town
cast shady underneath
laden clouds, day glo signs
the dented hood of this car
that broke my legs
and the snow falls

...
...
.

I can hear college girls
in the corner
huddled over bestickered laptops
"...that guy over there..."
"...he needs to get laid..."
the coffee stands up for me
although
my chest is bending at the bars
foolishly protecting
a heart fixed on
beating to death

Thump.
Thump.

Thump.

my fingers grip things
I can't seem to see

hand holds
mind folds
this wallet is getting lighter
and this pen is starting
to slip across a page
atop 1000's of blank pages
soon to be filled
with pretty words
about a face
gone
snapped into memory
between two severed wings
floating lazily to some kind of bottom
no plane will take you to.

Tick tock, Sanborn.

Tick.
Tock.

Just means it was real, right? Right?

It's alright, my friend
to question why
and wake up trying to understand
so late in the game
what happened
and how
it just says that you swam
balls out with sharks
rather than toeing the water
from the boat

idling while dreaming,
watching while whittling.

It's alright, my friend
to lament the reproach
of a woman turned to
spite and spittle
that once carried a torch
somewhere between her heart
and her ass
beckoning the livelihood
dreams
and insatiable hope
that defines you.

It's alright.

Now go back to bed.

1010 NW 17th

The footfalls come steady, echoing off the walls that swiftly
slit by, vibrant enough to overpower the small ear buds
nestled in his ears like ripe black berries. The blood that
lances through his veins has been transformed into ambrosia,
a sweet nectar that his teeth can taste inside their enamel
castles. As people pass he can smell them. Their fear, their
unwashed hair prickling at the base of their pale necks, their

needless strain trying to float among the middle of the sidewalk. He can smell their muddy dreams, as broken as his own.

A wise man once told him not to run from wolves, but rather to chase them. Whether this aged man was a product of his imagination or a true seer of old the young man could not remember. Yet such advice he follows, his eyes burning like cold blue fire and every muscle taut from the thrill of the hunt. As the hills rise in challenge he crests them, seeming to gain strength as he nears the top. There is something ancient and mystical about the traversal of a small hill. The man loses track of the connection between himself and the soil that will someday consume him. Perhaps this is a result of the impermanence of his step. Like every runner the man seeks to quiet his footfalls and keep himself aloft as long as possible.

Someday I will fly.

As he cuts through the parked cars and stolen bicycles the night envelopes him like a cold wind off the river. The breeze cools his burning skin, no doubt a product of the lack of melanin deep below his pores and the soft pink saran wrap that lies above. The man is dressed darkly, less a choice of style and more of necessity, yet foolish nonetheless. No car will stop for a jet-black, sinewy wolf pouncing in front of it. A man would be a fool even to slow down.

Where is my fur?

The skin-tight running clothes only cling to the skin, offering no protection from tooth or claw. The minimal shoes cut into the soles. They are training pads, moleskin coasters atop half-drunk cocktails. I wasn't just born in the wrong place and time.

I was born the wrong animal.

As he passes the bars, overflowing with excited shrieks and the intoxicating smells of the Meat Market, he hurries along lest he be sucked into the gape and awe. He worries of what would happen if he lingered. If he became entranced.

White wolves hunt alone.

These sidewalks are the fringe, the Industrial District, the perfect grounds to get lost in. While the blocks are filled with the wickedest of pollutants, streaming from factories that only operate at night, the area is nonetheless ringed with a resolute forest. The man used to love getting lost in the thick underbrush and dwarfing hills. Until his knees, ankles and feet decided that they were against such revelry. Now the man sticks to the 'even' ground, as if such a thing exists in this city, tackling the small hills as he dreams of cresting much, much higher. Mountains of scree and bleached, blanched undergrowth. Pinnacles.

The man suddenly remembers a glorious afternoon where he took flight into the woods. The morning dew had just left the ferns, arms still heavily drooped with the cold reminders of the night, and the stream raged amongst the narrow confines of the gulch. The water threatened to take over the narrow pathway and envelop the man-made structures keeping the area habitable. Runnable. As the water careened into the corners of the man-made turns the water jutted into the sky as if defiant. The man remembered coming to the moss-covered castle that he had once taken Her, at which point he turned around and raced the bulging stream down the course of the hill. The man had always had bad knees but that day, the sun beaming in the heart of winter with a glorious splendor reminiscent of a summer's day, he raced the miles down the gulch with a child's enthusiasm. Twice he almost fell, a fate that would have sealed his own without a doubt. Yet when he reached the bottom his adrenaline carried him to the steps of the steel bridge. The man remembered bellowing to the regal sun. His eyes locked with that which gives life to this teraqueus speck of dust. With a sad smile the man shakes his head, picking up the pace to drown out the memories of a time not long past, yet centuries ago.

The man snaps out of his reverie as his foot pops, a gut-wrenching feeling of warmth and detachment that shoots pain up his spine like an icy needle three feet long. This causes him to instinctively jump in the air, eyes flaring, his mouth growling. When he alit on the ground he felt a similar, yet diminished, twinge in his knees.

I'm broken.

The man knew of his ailments. They had plagued him for years. Evidently the cure was to avoid such exercise. Get a gym. Ride a bike. Ingratiate.

Fuck that.

Still, as the pain coursed through his veins the man was forced to consider it. He did not stop, however, grimacing when he was sure no one was looking and favoring the other leg to carry him home. He looked at the street signs. One mile left.

Till it falls off.

Just then a gaggle of beautiful women rounded the corner in front of him, a sight that always made his shoulders rear up in pride. His eyes lit from coals to a desire as hot as the inside of several supernovae. As the man passed he forced a quick smile and nod, then swept around the next corner as fast as he could. From the corner of his eye he could see a pretty brunette watching him go. The man had seen her around the neighborhood, in coffee shops and on the streetcar. He had never said hello and neither had she. He knew, she knew. Yet the man went home alone. His knee began to burn and flare.

As he looked up to the clouds, for guidance or in spite no one will ever know, the man suddenly knew just what it was that had always made him different; just what it was that drew him to the streets at night; just what it was that kept him on the fringes. His blood was different. They could not smell it. He could.

Probably better that way.

As fast as lightning a hole appeared in the thick gray blanket of clouds hovering over the city. The moon appeared, half-full and waning. The man began to howl.

the motions

I write the same
poem
over and over
telling inside jokes to
myself and placating some
inherent desire
to put everything
down on
screen.

what a life i've
given myself.

Fin says that
the things that keep me alone
keep me alive.
ironic
isn't it,
the slow death digging
its way into your spine
is the result of
your own
attempts to stay alive.

hilarious.

maybe I should write
another
poem
about it.

lineage

the hatred of silence
the loneliness that echoes
like a room still quivering
after roars and slammed doors
I know now
where the emptiness
comes from.
It is the feeling

of having had it all
for just a moment
of seeing the flash
the flame, the flickering
blue light irradiating
everything you've ever wanted:
a family
now these places
that hollow pit inside
your chest
you've tried to fill
fill, fill
the need for someone to
'understand'
to love you
all comes clearly
to the forefront
always there
behind the haze and smog
I remember leaving
those last moments
always on porches
always shaking hands
loose connections
with too-open arms
foreign couches
"just for a few weeks"
my mother looking back into
the back seat
with a strained optimism
that I see now
in the mirror
so often.
This is why I can't stay.
I cannot bear to watch
them leave
I cannot let them slowly in
only to have them creep

quickly out
as I am left
with dull memories and realities
of how
my entire life
has been lived with a bag packed
ready for "Dad's turn"
then "back to Mom's"
then "I'm moving again"
"far this time"
then "You're going to spend some time away"
then "I'm not coming back
this time"
then
fuck it.

and I see it all now
so crystal clear
that need to move, move, move
to see it all
and where once
I was afraid of not
seeing enough
now, I know
the true fear
the horror in the back
of my mind
is what I will do
when I finally, finally
don't want to run anymore
when I've seen enough
and where I can
if it exists
find the strength
to go back to that city
where they all walked away
and try to make a stand
still hearing the sounds

of latches and scuffling feet
resolutely
not moving.

kinetic

Fuck that.
I've spent my waking existence
tempering, forging, maladapting
and from a chalky white coke
I have emerged as a glistening
impossibly sharp longsword.

I am ready.
And you insolent little fucks
think you know something.

I've spent my whole life trying
to prove
that you don't, that you have no idea,
that you and I are one and the same,
that 2 and 2 isn't necessarily
addition.

A writer holds the voice
in the palm of his hand in a vice grip,
the repeatedly shattered bones of his hand
the evidence of primitive observations
and obfuscations
made against air, cement, the gamut
of suitable planks and, of course,
stalwart bones
we break so easily.

Now I must remove from the stew
in my mind's crock pot and serve up
healthy portions.
Here is a steaming bowl of your own
regurgitated bullshit. Enjoy. Sir.

Here is the scathing truth.

Here is my hand.

Hold it and we all just might
make it out of this place
pulverized smiles
somewhat intact.

Here I sit, crouched against the window pane, still reeling. I'm in the growing pains of an extended childhood that lingers. I am simply the smell of spilled diesel inside an old Toyota adamantly drawing rapt attention. Next to my arm stands a Devil, the same pitiful beast who once glared back into my eyes and smirked as I offered her my soul. The offer was a simple exchange: one soul for one forgotten lifetime. I naively assumed that this was a bargain.

I had thought that even a fool could not ignore such an opportunity. This wretched creature had the tenacity to consider the deal, weighing the shreds in one hand as strain etched deep furrows in her ominously beautiful face. Eventually her strength gave and she dropped it on the ground, obviously struggling to contain herself. She had passed. She turned quickly away on one foot, softly treading down the railroad we had been standing upon. Over her shoulder she murmured something that became scarred in my memory. Constantly ringing between my ears every night as I try to regain a lifetime's worth of sleep.

"Good luck, Sam. I'll be seeing you."

Now this trenchant creature, nonchalantly dressed in a white overcoat, is back. Her middle is slashed with a bright sash and bluntly trimmed with the same garish shade of prime red. She sits, gaily, next to my arm. She looks up at me with head cocked. Ever so invitingly.

"Give it up, Sam. You could never hack it and you never will."

The back of my mind screams in agreement. My wiry frame is stretched close to snapping with a boiling ache of longing. My balls hide inside my jeans as if shy.

My fingers move.

I latch onto the cold skin, a condensed cold clinging to the outside of every small white hair. She tries to laugh but is quickly silenced by the quick steps toward the kitchen. Then the screaming begins.

"SAM. YOU HAVE NO CHANCE. YOU'RE NOTHING. YOU'LL NEV..."

And I break her neck, calmly pouring the bottle out into the polished stainless steel sink burrowed into the cabinets. Her blood smells like poison and my nostrils begin to plead, but I've never been able to hear that well anyway.

I never asked to be born and I sure as hell never signed a contract.

That doesn't mean I have to negotiate.

11 cents

this whole charade
gets colder as you get older
the decisions cast across
pre-painted canvasses
hold more weight on your sore neck
and shame becomes something
finally measurable in failures
compounded as interest.
This ink doesn't move quite
as well as the rain falls
on a bed of bags and grass
summer is late here
and the humid peace of
such days
seems blatantly unattainable
as the gray clouds
slowly obscuring a fading dream
reality set in long ago
but you never heeded the warnings
choosing instead to gallivant spectacular
drinking cheap beer like champagne
telling grandiose stories about mundane events
flitting from bus to bus
thumb out
as if researching the human experience.
That's what you convinced yourself of.
No amount of self-pity or loathing
will keep you warm tonight
and there is certainly no massive check
on its way in an immaculate, muscled
black sedan
you are plainly out in the cold
hoping for a bail out

with so many bills
just the human embodiment
of American indebtedness
and you get older, older, older still
decisions mostly awful
and cast across a now-dented
punched-through canvass
'cause you were too naive and stubborn
to read the writing, hear the wind
and take off the mask of your charade
before you were this cold.

<u>choked up</u>

Remember when
poems were the end all
to the be all
and two hundred words
were way more
than that?

Remember when waking
was a transcendental experience
free from shame,
a behaviorally driven to-do list
and the coffee and eggs
you've had 1000's of times?

It's a long held under
standing
that the suffering inherent
in existing is the engine

that could
prompt and promote
strong stanzas
and emotive meanings
but as you get older
it's easier
you've learned to alleviate
through corrosive methods
and habits
and the words just don't find their way
to paper anymore.

i might be done with this poetry.

for years
this
has been the primary medium
for my sublimation.
for my loneliness.
in these perforated pages
i have found an encompassing
solace, a temporary reprieve
with words and phrases
i've been able to clear myself
a path through the muck
of wilderness that is a
reactionary persona clinging to
stubbornness.

now,
with the water licking the edges of my
cragged face
i can hardly brace myself
for the tumult of message
i've grown older
yet somehow less clarified
for now,
wisdom lies in the knowledge that
black and white are simply
shades of gray
and humility is what is left
in the middle.

i'm not a wreck of yesterday
i'm not a fool of tomorrow
and i'm not
for damn sure

going to wallow anymore.

it's a new day with the same sun
and i need no dramatic crutch.
this written
has ceased to enlighten me,
and i refuse to repeat myself
needlessly.

goodbye poetry.
i owe you only what i've
given you
which is the self-gratification
of finishing something tenuous
yet valuable.

and i think i can
finally
live with that.

Onwards.

Made in the USA
Charleston, SC
08 November 2015